C000132721

AIDS
A Christian Handbook

AIDS

A Christian Handbook

Colin E. Crowther

EPWORTH PRESS

British Library Cataloguing in Publication Data

Crowther, Colin E.
AIDS
1. Man. AIDS – Christian viewpoints
I. Title
261.561

ISBN 0–7162–0472–X

First published 1991
by Epworth Press
1 Central Buildings, Westminster,
London SW1H 9NR

Phototypeset by Input Typesetting Ltd
and printed in Great Britain by
Billing & Sons Ltd, Worcester

Contents

Acknowledgments   vii

Preface   ix

A Word about Words   xi

Part One · LOVING GOD

Introduction   3
Why there's no single theological answer   3
AIDS is God's curse on homosexuals   6
AIDS is God's punishment on an immoral generation   10
AIDS is an example of evil in the world   14
AIDS shows up our lovelessness   16
AIDS and the God of love   20
Material for prayer and reflection   32

Part Two · LOVING OURSELVES

Introduction   39
Loving our weakness   40
Loving our feelings   49
Loving our fears   53
Material for prayer and reflection   65

Part Three · LOVING OTHERS

Introduction   71
Coming together   72
What can Christians do together?   76
What can Christians do individually?   83
What will be distinctive about our Christian service?   90
Homelessness   90
Suicide   93

Hospital visiting   98
Material for prayer and reflection   108

Part Four · LETTING OTHERS LOVE US

Introduction   113
Letting others love us   113
Material for prayer and reflection   117

Part Five · LETTING GOD LOVE US

Introduction   123
Letting God love us   123
Material for prayer and reflection   141

Acknowledgments

There are so many people whose lives and words have inspired me in my work in this area that it would be impossible to acknowledge them all, but to the Revd Carolyn Henson and to Dr Bernard Rattigan my especial thanks are due, not only for their painstaking criticism of this book in the various stages of its development, but also for their constant enthusiasm and encouragement.

I am grateful to the following publishers for permission to quote their copyright material:

Cairns Publications, for permission to quote from *Healing – More or Less* by Jim Cotter, 2nd edn 1990

Darton, Longman & Todd Ltd, for permission to quote from *AIDS: Sharing the Pain* published and copyright 1988 by Darton, Longman and Todd Ltd.

St Paul Publications, for permission to quote from *AIDS: Meeting the Community Challenge*, 1987.

World Council of Churches, Programme Unit on Faith Witness, for permission to quote from the Church & Society Document, *AIDS and the Church*.

All Bible quotations are from the New English Bible Second Edition © 1970, by permission of Oxford and Cambridge University Presses.

Preface

To help you decide if this book is for you

The aim of this book is to challenge, enable and empower Christians to become compassionately involved in service to people with HIV infection and AIDS, and to support their friends and families.
 – If you don't know what you think about AIDS
 – If you feel you ought to be doing something but you don't know what
 – If you want to do something but feel totally inadequate to the task and don't know where to start
 – If you are passionately concerned about people with AIDS and want to find a way of sharing your concern with your Christian friends
then this book is written for you.
The book assumes you know no more about HIV or AIDS than you have picked up through the media and no more about theology than you have heard in sermons.

It isn't an ordinary book and it isn't an easy book. It will make you think again about what you know of God, what you think of yourself and what you feel about people who may be very different from you.

The book has been designed to be flexible, recognizing that everyone has a different need and a different starting point. You can read it on your own. Or you can read one section alone and then meet with a group of Christian friends and discuss it. Some church groups may want to use the book as an adult study course, possibly for Lent. Others may wish to use parts of the book in workshops with other Christian groups.

It is hoped that whether you've only just started to think about

AIDS or whether you have already spent some time working alongside people with AIDS, you will find something here to challenge you to reassess how you feel, to enable you to decide what to do about it and to empower you with the confidence and conviction to translate good intentions into caring actions.

Anyone who has worked with people affected by AIDS will tell you that once one breaks through one's own barriers of fear and ignorance, one discovers that this is no morbid and depressing business but a real privilege. What one learns from people with AIDS is inspiring and enriching.

So, finally, this is not just a book about AIDS, but about all human suffering and all human potential, leading us into a deeper experience of God's love for us and giving us, perhaps for the first time, the means to love ourselves and others as he loves us.

A Word about Words . . .

The words we use describe not only what we are discussing but also how we feel about it. Observing the same group of people, one person may speak of them as 'football supporters' while another speaks of 'football hooligans'. The difference between these two people lies in their attitude towards the people they have both seen.

Similarly, to speak of people 'dying of AIDS' or of people 'living with AIDS' reveals how we feel about them and what we think is happening to them.

None of this would matter very much if it were not for the way in which the human mind works. Even the most casual remark, constantly repeated, will build into an attitude and that attitude will soon set into a prejudice which will prevent us thinking freshly and freely. Hardening the mind is the first step to hardening the heart.

But our choice of words not only helps reflect and form our attitude, it also helps us to attract people who think like us and to repel people who do not. In the company of like-minded people (and we all choose to speak to like-minded people), we take short-cuts with language and end up speaking in a sort of code called jargon.

Because we spend most of our time talking to people who think like us, we easily fall into the mistake of assuming everyone knows what we mean and that everyone thinks like us.

For example, between Christians, words like redemption, sin and incarnation have a particular meaning, whereas non-Christians hearing these words will not only look blank, they will also 'cut off', feeling alienated and angry at our inability to translate what we mean into terms that have meaning for them. So taking short-cuts with language and using jargon can distance us both from new ideas and from new people.

Theological jargon, of course, is not the only kind. Medical jargon is just as alienating and meaningless to people not used to it.

If you already know a bit about AIDS, you will recognize (even if you do not understand) terms like AB+, HIV+, BP, ARC, AIDS or PLWAS. To most people these linguistic shortcuts mean nothing and only serve to reinforce the idea that AIDS is too technical for ordinary mortals and should be left to the theologians and healers.

Yet we are all theologians. We all ask who God is and how he feels about us and about our world. We are all healers. Our words and actions can wound, weaken and destroy just as much as any virus. Or they can soothe, strengthen and revitalize, just as much as any tranquilizer, anti-biotic or 'cure'.

So using the right words is important, not simply in our desire to understand and express truth, but also because words are so powerful. Despite what the children's rhyme says, we all know that words have caused more hurt than any number of sticks and stones.

In the course of this book most of the abbreviations and coded phrases used around AIDS will be examined and explained, but it might help to take just one example now.

Superficially, AB+, HIV+ and BP seem to be saying the same thing. AB+ = antibody positive, which means that a sample of blood was tested and found to have begun to fight off the human immuno-deficiency virus that can cause AIDS. HIV+ means the same thing – it just describes more accurately to which virus the blood sample has begun to react. BP = Body Positive and you may be forgiven for assuming this is just a simplification of both AB+ and HIV+. It isn't.

BP describes not a sample of blood, but the person from whom that sample came. It does describe the 'HIV-status' of that person: their blood, when tested, showed a positive result, whereas blood from someone who had not been exposed to the virus which can cause AIDS would have shown negative.

But BP does more than describe a person and their[1] HIV-status. It describes how they feel about it. Their reaction is a positive one. They are concerned not just with the Antibody but with their whole Body. They know that they are at risk of developing AIDS, but

[1] I am deliberately using their, they, etc, even though I am writing in the singular, to avoid having to choose between he and she. If I used he, your preconceived idea that AIDS is a gay disease and that gays are men would be reinforced. If I used she, you might not believe me.

equally they know that at the moment they are feeling fit and healthy. They have not got AIDS. They may never get AIDS. They do not know the future anymore than anyone else does. What concerns them is how to stay healthy.

BP means more even than that. Just as for Christians the word body has several meanings – Jesus as the bread of Life, the church as his body on earth – so Body Positive has several layers of meaning. It can refer not just to individuals and their concern to protect and nurture their own health, but also to their identifying themselves with other people in the same situation.

In this sense, BP is that body or group of people who share a common concern to support one another as together they wait, in a positive frame of mind, to see what the future will bring.

Now that you know all that, you probably feel differently about the terms AB+, HIV+ and BP. You will find yourself starting to use them with confidence. But think how many people you know who still neither know nor want to know what these terms mean. What will be the effect on you and on them of your using jargon?

The dangers of jargon

1. You can feel that once you have mastered the jargon you are half-way to becoming an expert. You *own* these phrases and expressions. They impress outsiders. Whether you intend it or not, outsiders will believe what you say about AIDS because you sound like a doctor.

Jargon helps to protect and disguise our ignorance.

2. Jargon also helps to distance painful subjects. It hurts to speak of Jane or Tom who have AIDS, so we talk instead of people with AIDS, we quote statistics on AIDS, or we write PLWAs (People Living With AIDS). Effectively, we are rubbing out the faces of real people and substituting shapes, numbers or letters. It helps to soften the blow and distance the reality. Yet our value as carers and our worth as a caring community depend precisely on our preparedness to hurt, to stay vulnerable and to think of Jane and Tom who have AIDS.

Jargon helps to protect and disguise our vulnerability.

3. Using jargon reflects and reinforces our search for quick and easy answers. We are careful to distinguish BP from PLWA, ignoring

the fact that every person living with AIDS is also body positive. We separate HIV from ARC and ARC from AIDS, deliberately blinding ourselves with science and ignoring the fact that someone who is body positive may or may not go on to develop one of that group of diseases associated with AIDS but which are not actually AIDS (which is what ARC means – AIDS-related complex). Or they may develop ARC and then go back to being perfectly well. Or they may go from ARC to AIDS or from HIV to AIDS.

Or they may stay perfectly well.

But it is as if we don't want to know that. It is as if the truth were too complicated and we prefer simplicity even when it is a simple lie.

Most of all, we can be told a million times that no one dies of AIDS and still not hear it. People with AIDS die of cancers. People with AIDS died of pneumonias. They are cancers and pneumonias which are in all of us but which only get out of hand when the HIV virus prevents our bodies' defence systems protecting us from them. AIDS is better thought of not as a disease so much as an explanation of why the body's immune system is sometimes not able to do its job of neutralizing potentially harmful diseases.

Even if you see AIDS as invariably fatal, this does not mean that AIDS is untreatable. Many diseases cannot be cured but they can be treated. AIDS is one. So is high blood pressure. In the same way, all the symptoms of AIDS can be treated so that in most cases the person with AIDS can enjoy a comfortable quality of life most of the time. Their life can be prolonged. Their hope can honestly be nurtured.

Using jargon helps to protect and disguise us from the truth (which if often more complex but more hopeful) by supplying us with the quick, easy answers we really want to hear, and prefer to believe, even if they are not true.

So know the jargon by all means. Use the short-cuts where they help you communicate accurately and quickly. But recognize them for what they are – barriers to our facing how little we know, how much we hurt, and how impatiently we want AIDS simply to go away.

Short-cuts though do sometimes have their uses. In a book like this, for instance, it would be impossibly irritating for the reader if I were to repeat a page-long definition of what I meant every time. Now that you have at least been alerted to the dangers, I can define what I mean by the 'shorthand' I will be using.

When I am referring to the disease, I will use the word AIDS. This is taken to include HIV infection and ARC.

When I am referring to people, I will use the phrase *people affected by AIDS*. That includes

– people who are body positive
– people who have ARC
– people who have AIDS
   – and those whom they love

in other words, everyone whose lives have in some way been affected by AIDS.

Even if we are not using jargon, our words can have a devastating effect if they are chosen carelessly. For example, you may have heard (and begun to copy) those who refer to 'people dying of AIDS' or to 'victims of AIDS'. Sometimes they are used interchangeably, as if they meant the same thing. But if jargon is really about self-delusion, then using these phrases is about projecting our self-delusion, fear and ignorance onto others – often with appalling effects. Careless talk does cost lives.

How?

Victims of AIDS

Because of the irresponsibility of members of the tabloid press (who did not observe the early and excellent advice of their own union, the NUJ), people (victims) of AIDS (the Gay Plague) are victims of our prejudice. But they may be seeing themselves, or being seen by others, as victims in other ways as well, so it is worth pausing for a moment to look at what victim can mean.

Victim can mean innocent bystander destroyed by an insensate primal element: the fisherman who is swept off the end of a pier by a tidal wave. The fear thus expressed may be that no one is safe from an alien and wilful chaos; that none of us is strong enough to resist the forces of a malignant nature. We could respond by withdrawing into ourselves and cutting ourselves off from other people because life is perceived as 'every one for himself'.

Victim can mean the chosen target of a malevolent and destructive will or force: an example would be the unsuspecting pedestrian who is knocked down by a car as soon as they step off the kerb. The response then could be one of paranoia that an unseen enemy is out to get you for an unknown reason. It is this fear which is fed by horror movies. Everyone becomes your potential enemy.

Victim can mean one unremarked and unremembered face in a crowd of other victims, mown down by an equally faceless crowd of oppressors. An obvious example would be concentration camp victims. What made them victims? The fact that they were the chosen target or the fact that they let themselves be treated like that? People become victims when they start to believe other people's propaganda against them. They see themselves as helpless because other people describe them that way. By such a reckoning, all that humanity has in common is the lowest common denominator of racial, religious or sexual orientation.

Victim can mean rightfully condemned person, awaiting their just execution: the picture then is of a condemned cell, halfway between the court and the gallows. In such a case the danger described is that of feeling that one merits the sentence of death. This is the person who says, 'People have always told me I don't deserve to live, now I believe them. Soon I will be dead and erased from the memory of those who never loved or accepted me. It will be as if I had never lived.'

There are of course many other ways of describing 'victims', but what they all have in common is the effect of regarding the persons so nominated as powerless to affect their fate. To call someone a victim is to give them a death sentence.

That is why we must always stop ourselves – and others – using this word. It allows us to distance ourselves from what we perceive as happening to them. It is also untrue: people with AIDS are not helpless.

Their attitude to themselves and to their illness will greatly affect how they experience either that illness or that possibly lifelong period of waiting to see if they do become ill. Since the way we regard ourselves is affected to a great extent by the way others regard us, the least we can do to people affected by AIDS is to help them see themselves honestly – and that means positively.

If enough people tell me I look ill, I begin to feel ill and eventually I become ill. If enough people tell me I'm a victim, I give up on myself and look only to the worst that could possibly happen to me.

Dying of AIDS or living with AIDS?

You might be forgiven for thinking that the difference between these is one of wishful thinking. To a healthy extent, that would be true. Our wishes very often do come true. If we expect to see a bright new tomorrow, the chances are we shall see one. It will be the same tomorrow which the pessimist sees, but the optimist will at least be able to enjoy the sunshine, ignored by the pessimist who is waiting for the showers. Whose day was better spent?

It is precisely because of the power of mind over matter, precisely because prognoses become self-fulfilling predictions, that doctors are reluctant sometimes to tell their patients what their medical experience has persuaded them is the likely terminal outcome of their physical condition.

It is not a matter of ignoring the certainty of death or of pretending that death will go away. It is not a matter of death at all. It is a matter of life. Many people with HIV, ARC and AIDS have already come to terms with their feelings about death. Many of them have come to see that what matters is not the length but the depth of life, not the quantity but the quality. They rightly insist that they are learning to live with AIDS; that having AIDS has provided them with an opportunity they might otherwise not have grasped to reassess what is important to them; to learn that what really matters is how we live each moment to the full; and to accept that the future is not ours to own or to predict. We have only this moment. We need only this moment.

Because so many of them have experienced (or expected) rejection from mainstream churches, they do not think in our jargon or express themselves in our language. But I would suggest that they are doing the same thing as any Christian is doing when Christians ponder in awe the idea of their being created in God's image and seek to follow Christ's precepts and find life's meaning not in success, riches or longevity, but in the intensity of their experience of the closeness of God and of the beautiful fragility of this existence.

For these reasons, careers always speak of a person living with AIDS.

1. It puts the person first.
2. It puts the emphasis on living.
3. It speaks in terms of harmony, of co-operation: *with* AIDS not *against* AIDS. The person with AIDS is not fighting against the clock. They are not engaged in murderous civil war against their own bodies. They are learning to treasure their body; to recognize its

needs; to love and tenderly serve those needs, yet not to let those needs dominate. They are telling themselves how much they love and value themselves and that this is a new adventure in which body, mind and spirit are exploring how to live in a new harmony.

As Christians, we have much to share with such people in their quest for life's meaning and in their enjoyment of life's fullness, but only if we can learn to speak a common language.

If we can free ourselves from the prejudices which underlie our choice of words, we shall be enabled to hear what people living with AIDS – and those whom they love – are really saying to us. We need to take out of our ears the cotton wool of jargon that we hoped would protect our vulnerability and the wax that distorts the painful accuracy of our hearing. Then at last we shall be able to discern Christ speaking through them.

It all comes down to a choice of words.

The choice is ours.

Loving God

Loving God

Introduction

This part of the book will help you decide how you think God feels about AIDS and where he stands in regard to people affected by AIDS. But why is it necessary? My experience over five years has been that non-Christians who are prejudiced against people with AIDS claim justification for their views from what they have heard Christians say. Most of the Christians I meet still believe AIDS does not affect them and that people with AIDS have brought it on themselves and are experiencing divine punishment.

So you will be offered the chance to compare five different understandings of AIDS, all of which claim to be Christian.

Then you will be challenged to decide what your own views are. You will also be enabled to understand how others feel and to explain to them why you feel differently. Finally you will be asked to think about what action should flow from your decision. The rest of this book will empower you to carry that decision into action.

Why there's no single theological answer

Christians and non-Christians alike are often puzzled as to why on any issue the Christian response is always so varied and often contradictory.

The reason is partly that Christianity is less a religion (in the popular sense of a set of rules) than a relationship. Unlike Islam or Hinduism, Christianity is not a book, it claims to be a revealed religion. Christ revealed the nature of God (John 1.18) and made his followers inheritors not of prescribed rules and regulations, but sons and daughters of a living Father (John 1.12, 13).

There is therefore a close parallel between what Christians think God wants them to say and do and what children think their parents want them to say and do: it will vary from child to child, depending on the closeness of their relationship with their parents and on their maturity. So there can be as many Christian answers as there are Christians. What is worrying is not that there could be so many but that there actually are so few. Most Christians do not think for themselves. They allow others to do their thinking for them. One way or another, they select someone to be their voice and to speak for them. This becomes dangerous when that person is assumed thereby to be God's voice and to be speaking on his behalf. We mistakenly assume that because he represents many Christians his voice is in some way more definitively 'God's' than anyone else's. It is somewhat like the TUC. The vote of one individual or of one small union is just as valid as the block vote of the biggest union, but the bigger voter often attracts more attention.

Of course God does speak to us through priests and through preachers, but he also speaks to us in the still small voice of private meditation and in the often stormy voices of our non-Christian neighbours.

One consequence of the human attempt to reduce God from absolute to constitutional monarch, capable of speaking to his people only through their elected representatives, is that Christian answers to contemporary moral issues tend to fall into groups along 'party lines'. Each party or group is looking for what God is saying, but they are expecting to find the answer in different places. One group will be looking for what God is likely to say, based on what he has said in the past. They will look in the Bible. Another group will look at what Christians have, over the years, considered to be 'God's line'. They will look to Christian tradition. A third group will be swayed by what eloquent individuals proclaim God is saying now, based on their assuming the prophets' mantle.

Of course this is an oversimplification, but it does demonstrate that the answer we get to a question depends on who we're asking and where we're expecting to find the answer.

But it isn't only the answers which vary. So do the questions. Very broadly speaking, the theological questions people ask about AIDS (the questions about God and his intentions to us and his will for us) fall into two categories.

If AIDS does not affect you personally, you will be looking at the issues from a different perspective than that of someone with AIDS. If you do not know much about AIDS, you will be framing your questions very differently from those of a parent whose son has just died as a result of AIDS.

So what we think about AIDS will depend on what we know about AIDS, and what we ask about AIDS will depend on how aware we are of the way in which AIDS is already affecting our lives. This list may help. If nothing else, it shows how different are the starting points of people whose lives AIDS has touched to a lesser or greater extent.

We ask	*They ask*
Why them?	Why me?
Why now?	If life expectancy doesn't mean threescore years and ten, what can I expect of life?
How should Christians respond to people with AIDS?	Why are so many Christians rejecting me personally? Why do the churches seem so silent and distant on this issue?
What is the Christian attitude to sex?	What gives them the right to 'love the sinner and hate the sin'? I can't help who I am. What sort of a God created me the way I am and then rejects me for being who I am?
What is the Christian attitude to death?	AIDS has taught me nothing about death but a lot about life. I have discovered that life is measured in moments not years and that what matters is the quality not the length of my life. Who will help me work out how to live so that I enjoy life to the full?
How can I pray for them?	I know I need to learn to live in loving harmony with my body and with what is happening to my body. I need to learn to recognize and develop my innate healing power and spiritual strength, how to love and value myself and to appreciate the beauty and usefulness of stillness. The Eastern religions have lots to say on this – what about Christians?

How can I serve them? Have Christians ever experienced this sense of peace and purpose I am discovering and exploring? Could we not share this? I have so much to teach and so much to learn. Will I ever find a Christian who has the humility to listen and the courage to face dark issues without prejudging them with worn-out jargon?

People who feel AIDS does not and will not affect them, will often feel that people with AIDS have brought it on themselves. Some will adopt a fundamentalist stance, using the Bible to support their belief and to allow them to distance themselves from the suffering of people with AIDS, suffering to which their condemnation has added considerably.

People whose experience of AIDS is more personal, or who see what happens to others as in some way happening to them as part of the family of humanity, will often adopt a liberal stance. Their questions will be asked not from the mountain-top looking down on the spectrum of human misery, but from the midst of that suffering, from the bedside of one of those whom the world and God seem to have rejected.

To help you decide where you stand on AIDS and where you think God stands, the following passages describe five theological positions on AIDS which people who claim to be Christian have adopted.

They start at one fundamentalist extreme and move gradually to one liberal extreme.

AIDS is God's curse on homosexuals

The most extreme fundamentalist position is to see AIDS as a curse visited by God on homosexuals. The argument, often with racial overtones, goes something like this:

'AIDS is a gay plague, borne by promiscuity from countries where blacks live. AIDS is a curse, visited by a just and vengeful God, on sexual deviants as a punishment for their deviance.'

Put more gently, the argument sounds like this:

'We thought we were doing the right thing in allowing blacks into our country; in allowing sexual deviance the right of expression; in becoming a permissive society. But Tolerance is not our God. Justice is. Gods does not tolerate this moral evil and nor should we. We must return to a Puritan ethic of white conformity, white chastity and white heterosexuality. Because evil is contagious, we must cut ourselves off from those visited by this affliction and see their suffering as a terrible warning to us all of the consequences of tolerating evil.'

Not every proponent of this approach would lay equal stress on the racial and sexual origins of this perceived evil. Some would stress inter-racial tolerance as the main cause. For others it would be tolerance of homosexuality. But these are changes only of emphasis which do not disguise the real root of this fundamentalist approach, which is the desire to find and brand a scapegoat; to divide the world into them and us, saved and sinners.

This argument needs to be looked at critically because it has been heard so often that it is in danger of creeping into everyone's attitudes unawares. The argument makes certain assumptions about the nature of God and about the nature of AIDS.

The first assumption is that ours is a God who curses. This has a very Old Testament feel to it, but, as I hope to show, no biblical foundation. Neither does it have any foundation in the Christian experience of God. But because the biblical passages put up to support this argument are taken from the Old Testament (or from Paul virtually quoting the Old Testament) I shall try to answer them using only Old Testament passages.

Seen as a whole, the Bible is the story of God's creation of us and of his desire to re-create us through his Son Jesus Christ. Ours is a God of creation, not destruction.

As we work through the Book of Genesis, we discover God creating humanity and then choosing to bind himself to us in a covenant. That covenant is not one of retribution but of mercy. The story of Noah exemplifies this.

Then Noah built an altar to the Lord, and took of every clean animal and of every clean bird, and offered burnt offerings on the altar. And when the Lord smelled the pleasing odour, the Lord said in his heart, 'I will never again curse the ground because of man, for the imagination of man's heart is evil from his youth; neither will I ever again destroy any living creature as I have done. While the earth remains, seedtime and harvest, cold and heat, summer and winter, day and night, shall not cease (Gen. 8.20–22).

Not only does this covenant give us the assurance of mercy, but of acceptance. God knows that 'the imagination of man's heart is evil from his youth' and yet still promises to be merciful to us. Nor is he a God who brings down curses on us:

Now the Lord said to Abram, 'Go from your country and your kindred and your father's house to the land that I will show you. And I will make of you a great nation, and I will bless you, and make your name great, so that you will be a blessing. I will bless those who bless you, and him who curses you I will curse; and by you all the families of the earth shall bless themselves' (Gen. 12.1–3).

The wonder of this passage is not simply that God offers us blessing, but the person through whom that blessing is passed on to us.

At this point in the story, Abram is a nobody, living obscurely in a place called Ur. Even his name is a joke, for Abram means 'exalted father' yet Abram has no children, is nearly a hundred years old and his wife is barren. It was as though God was purposely choosing someone insignificant in the world's eyes, possibly a failure, certainly a laughing-stock, in order to demonstrate the fact that though none of us is worthy to be chosen by him, he still loves and chooses us all to be his own.

So ours is a God of creation not destruction, a God who, knowing our weak nature and our propensity for evil, yet chooses to identify himself with us and offering to even the least of us acceptance, mercy and blessing.

So much for the assumptions about God which lie behind the 'curse of God' theory. What about the assumptions about AIDS?

The assumption is that AIDS only attacks homosexuals. Certainly, in the West, male homosexuals who engage in certain types of sexual activity have been at high risk. But female homosexuals (lesbians) are least at risk.

Those who believe that AIDS is God's curse on homosexuals have not faced up to this problem. Are they saying that God, like Queen

Victoria, refused to believe such women exist? Is God a male chauvinist? Or are female homosexuals less abhorrent to him than male homosexuals? If so, why?

If AIDS is indeed the Lord's own plague-sword, he presumably wields it with care to attack only those on whom his wrath has fallen, just as the angel of death only struck down the Egyptians and passed over the Israelites. But is this what is really happening?

The World Health Organization has been gathering statistics on AIDS for some time. Their figures show that, world-wide, AIDS has been responsible for a roughly equal number of male and female deaths; that AIDS is a disease affecting far more heterosexuals than homosexuals; it affects children as well as adults, rich as well as poor, women as well as men. If AIDS is indeed God's plague-sword, it has a very blunt and undiscriminating edge.

Or perhaps AIDS is not only God's curse on homosexuals but also his punishment on those societies who tolerate homosexuals. What do we know about the origins and means of transmission of the virus that can help us trace a possible path for God's angel of death?

The AIDS virus may have been around for a long time, possibly carried in a benign form in the blood of animals, suddenly and for an unknown reason becoming malignant in them, or becoming malignant when passed by them to humans. This seems to be the most widely-supported scientific opinion at the moment, though it must be stressed that it is only an opinion, not a fact; and the opinion of the moment, and not the final judgment on the issue.

So, the AIDS virus is in a little green monkey in Central Africa. God knows this. God is sick and tired of the behaviour of a certain gay man in Britain (or of all gay men in Britain), so he tells the little green monkey to bite a passing African man, when they meet one day in the African's fields. This is a fairly common occurrence. Being bitten by monkeys, especially when harvesting, is one of the dangers of being a Central African farmer – except, of course, that it's more likely to be a woman doing the hard work of harvesting.

The farmer and his wife have sex. One or other of them infects their unborn child, who grows up, marries another Central African farmer, has sex with him and infects him. She dies. He marries again and infects his new wife before he dies and she marries again. Or, even more likely, she is having trouble making a living off the poor land, so she goes to the city where there is no work but a lot of white tourists willing to pay her good money for sex. She agrees and has sex with a white American, who, when he returns home, has sex with his wife who subsequently donates blood which is infected and which is used to give a blood transfusion to a gay American man recovering from a car accident. This gay American man has sex with his partner. Their relationship eventually falls apart because of the strain of being a gay couple in America, or because they have now grown out of love with each other, and both go off to look for new relationships with different people, one of whom turns out to be a British tourist. This British tourist becomes infected, returns home, infects his British partner . . . who is the particular gay man God had it in for in the first place.

Are we really expected to take this as a serious scenario? It is certainly a quite credible scenario for the spread of the disease. But as a scenario for a curse sent by God to punish one or more gay British men, it is laughable.

Worse than that, it paints a picture of God so devious and nasty as to be literally beyond belief. Surely, if God wanted to punish gay men as a warning to the rest of us (either not to be gay men or not to tolerate them), he would have chosen a clearer path of cause and effect?

The extreme fundamentalist position, I suggest, is untenable. AIDS cannot be God's curse on homosexuals because ours is a God who blesses not curses, who knows our weaknesses and yet chooses to bind himself to us in loving mercy. And AIDS does not just kill homosexuals. Many homosexuals remain untouched by AIDS.

But what do you think? What is your experience of God? What do you expect God will do to you when something goes wrong in your life? Do you see the mess you are in as an expression of God's anger with you? Or do you feel you are reaping the result of what you have sown? If AIDS is not a curse sent by God, is it perhaps a punishment?

AIDS is God's punishment on an immoral generation

This very popular argument is best expressed in the words of Cardinal Archbishop Hume:

> . . . AIDS is neither the problem nor the central issue. It is a

symptom of something deeper and more deadly. AIDS is but one of the many disastrous consequences of promiscuous sexual behaviour. Promiscuity is the root-cause of the present epidemic. It has always been sinful; it is rapidly becoming suicidal.

The Times, 7 January 1987.

Those who support this argument are making several wild assumptions. The first is that because AIDS – in this country – is spread mainly by sexual contact, that this pattern is true throughout the world. There is no evidence for this. The second is that because AIDS can be transmitted sexually, it is always the result of promiscuity. There is no evidence for this. The third is to assume that it is permissible to turn human suffering into sermon-fodder. Those who do so need to be careful of the effect of their words both on people trying to live with this disease and on the rest of us who are trying to work out how we should respond to them.

Since most people with AIDS cannot point to how they acquired the virus, it ill behoves anyone else to do the pointing for them. If there are lessons to be learnt from AIDS, why do we assume they are negative ones? Why do we assume AIDS is about sin? Is it an appropriate Christian response to suffering to brand the sufferers as sinners and to hold them up as a dreadful warning to the rest of us?

Christians should be aware of their membership of a world family. Our statements on anything which affects our world family should reflect the totality of our experience of that problem and not just argue from local experience to global explanation. This is particularly true of AIDS which is affecting people in most countries of the world.

We need to start by taking on board the sum total of human knowledge of AIDS and human experience of AIDS. Our knowledge of AIDS is very partial still, but there is more than enough evidence already to show that AIDS affects us all: heterosexual and homosexual, man and woman, adult and child. Our experience of AIDS is that whenever Christians come alongside people living with the disease they find they have much to learn and little to preach, much to repent and little to teach, everything to praise and nothing to condemn.

Christians need to wait till they know more about how God is working in and through people with AIDS before they issue blanket condemnations which can misrepresent God, mislead his followers and add an intolerable burden to the suffering of people affected by AIDS.

Let's put their argument another way:

'God has laid down laws not for his sake but for ours. When these laws are followed, they result in our health and happiness. When they are broken, the resulting damage to our lives is self-inflicted. God told us what would happen if we broke his laws. We broke them. So we must suffer the consequences. AIDS is simply the particular punishment from God for promiscuity.'

Still this argument makes certain assumptions about God and about AIDS.

God, it assumes, works on a tit-for-tat basis. Do this and you'll get a sweetie. Do that and you'll get a thump. Follow my rules and you'll come to heaven. Follow your own and you'll go to hell.

Appealing as it is to our quest for quick, easy answers, does the picture this paints of God stand up beside the one Jesus painted of a shepherd who will risk his own life and the lives of the ninety-nine sheep already in his fold for one sheep that has gone astray?

If God really is the Father who loves us and who gives his children what he knows they need, surely his punishment of us is meant for our correction not for our destruction? How can I learn to correct my ways if I'm dead? How can I learn to love God if he's killed me?

And if AIDS is God's punishment for promiscuity, why didn't he tell me so? Why didn't he explain that if I was promiscuous (and very unlucky) in the 1960s I would get a course of anti-biotics for VD, but if I was promiscuous (and very unlucky) in the 1990s I would die of AIDS?

Such an approach leads easily to a mathematical understanding of divine justice, with every sin carefully graded and God, like the Mikado, making the punishment fit the crime. The fault surely lies not with God's justice but with our understanding of it. Ignoring the fact that it is impossible to be sure how anyone with AIDS acquired it, some of us are prepared to divide people with AIDS into innocent and guilty. The guilty are those who acquired AIDS by their own actions. Not only does this lead to us judging and condemning others, which the Bible expressly forbids us to do, it makes a mockery of his justice. For if God is punishing the guilty, he cannot in justice also punish the innocent. And if we are punishing ourselves, it must be for a sin we know we are committing or we have not been able to exercise moral choice and therefore cannot be held guilty of making the wrong choice.

But the known facts of AIDS transmission show that people infected with the virus which can cause AIDS are normally unaware that they are at risk and hence are unaware that they are putting anyone else at risk. The known facts of AIDS transmission show that in many cases people with AIDS have acquired it as the result of someone else's 'sin'. The child has acquired it from her mother. The haemophiliac has acquired it from untreated blood or blood products. The African family has acquired it by seeking to protect their health in getting vaccinated against other potentially fatal disease, unaware of the risks of shared needles. By any scale of justice, most people with AIDS acquired it unwittingly and innocently and pass on the virus which can cause AIDS unwittingly and therefore innocently.

If we release AIDS from the puritannical corset of this type of sexual morality, and see it in the wider context of divine justice, larger and more important issues are raised.

In the case of a Scottish teenager who acquired AIDS, he thinks, by sharing a needle when injecting heroin, what sin are we talking about? His sin is in abusing instead of respecting his body as the temple of the Holy Spirit? Or our sin for our part in a society in which young people often have no prospect of work and hence no sense of belonging or contributing to our society; no money and hence no means to acquire the security of a place of their own; no hope that our world will ever be one in which they shall want to take part? For too many young people, life is something they seek to escape from rather than embrace with confidence. We all surely share responsibility with them for that. When a teenager injects drugs, one of the things he is doing is to try to inoculate himself against us.

Or take the case of the Ugandan child who acquired AIDS, her mother thinks, when she was vaccinated against a serious childhood illness by a government health worker who used the same needle over and over again until it was blunt. Is the mother to blame for wanting to protect her child against one disease only to see her die of another? Is the health worker to blame, who probably knew that the practice of using needles more than once was risky for many reasons? Or is the Ugandan government to blame for not having enough money to buy enough needles from Western countries? Or are Western countries to blame for building their own wealth by keeping Third World countries poor? We have the technology but have not shared it. We offer the Third World at best charity but not equality, our left-overs but not justice.

AIDS does indeed raise questions of justice but they rebound on our own heads. Promiscuity is not the root-cause of the spread of AIDS, but the injustice of world poverty.

So to those who believe that AIDS is a punishment either from God or from themselves for sexual promiscuity, there are some serious questions still to be answered:

– On what grounds do you assume that AIDS is only spread by promiscuous sexual contact?

– If you accept that AIDS is spread in many different ways, on what grounds do you ignore the biblical prohibition against judging others and divide people with AIDS into innocent and guilty 'victims'?

– Of what are these people victims? God's erring justice or your erring judgment?

– What is the effect on people of AIDS of your blanket condemnation of them as having been promiscuous?

– Why is God punishing sexual promiscuity so hard – and only in this generation?

– Is the root-cause of AIDS a matter of sexual morality or human injustice?

AIDS is an example of the evil in the world

If God is not the source of the curse which you might still feel is on AIDS, what is? Could it be that the disease itself is evil?

What do we know about the AIDS virus? The first thing is that it is hidden. The number of reported cases of AIDS is still quite small. One reason for this is the reluctance of some governments to admit to having any cases at all in case such a revelation harms its tourist or other interests. The result is that these countries deny AIDS is a problem for them or they deliberately massage the figures down to unremarkable levels. Another reason is that some countries just do not have the means or the resources to stop caring for the dying long enough to count them.

But the main reason is that no one knows. The number of AIDS cases today reflects the extent of the spread of AIDS over five years ago, because the incubation period for the virus is often at least as long as that. To say, for example, that AIDS in England affects mainly gay or bisexual men is misleading: what the statement really means is that the number of AIDS cases in England today suggests that over five years ago the virus had spread widely among gay and bisexual men. It gives us no grounds whatsoever for assuming they are the group most affected today.

The fact that the full truth about the extent of the spread of AIDS is not known is being used by many of us to pretend or to hope that it will go away. But Dr Jonathan Mann of the World Health Organization, giving evidence to the World Council of Churches Hearing on AIDS, had this to say:

> People want so terribly to believe that this disease will not affect them. I wish it were true. The evidence is clear. This disease is spreading rapidly into parts of the world where it did not exist before and it is spreading and becoming more serious in those parts of the world in which it is already present.
>
> *AIDS and the Church*, p. 8.

So one reason for the hidden nature of AIDS is our desire to hide from it.

But there is another remarkable feature of the AIDS virus, and that is its fragility. Virulent inside the body, some medical experts believe it dies almost instantly outside the body. It is extraordinary that the world is standing in awe and dread of something so tiny and frail. Furthermore, this tiny, frail, hidden virus depends for its transmission on the closest intimacy. John Habgood, Archbishop of York, expresses it thus:

> The Aids virus is fragile. For its transmission it depends upon intimate contact. And there is an interesting connection between intimacy and vulnerability. Every intimate contact makes us vulnerable in all sorts of ways not only through transmission of infection but also psychologically and in our personal identity. And this is why every civilization has in its various ways surrounded intimate relationships with rules, with structures, with ceremonies, with taboos. These have as it were protected the

relationships. And that is why I see the AIDS epidemic as teaching us that we cannot lightly treat these intimate relationships any longer. And that is where the world has lost its sense that close contact between human beings needs to be within an ordered framework. Then it is sure to recover that perspective. And this it seems to me is a moral and theological understanding which can be expressed in ways which are accessible not only to those with Christian commitment but to all those who think seriously about our human nature and our contacts with one another.

AIDS and the Church, p. 19.

AIDS is not evil. It is not a malignant force. AIDS is no more than a tiny, fragile virus. It is morally neutral. Its significance theologically lies in what it reveals about us through our reactions to it. It needs us as much as we need each other. It needs our intimacy with each other as much as we need that intimacy. And in that intimacy it is as vulnerable as we are.

AIDS shows up our lovelessness

In our reactions to the disease and in our assumptions about God we have seen reflections of the real curse, reflections of ourselves.

In the face of something new we have assumed it to be evil. Presented with something unknown we have been unable to live with the not-knowing and have filled the gaps in our knowledge and understanding with our most deep-rooted prejudices and fears. Thus we have compounded our fears and in blind panic have sought not a solution but a scapegoat.

It is therefore not AIDS we need to address but those fears which AIDS has reawakened in us, fears so great that even we who believe in a God in whom everything works to our good can see nothing but divine retribution.

The first of our fears is of contagion. This is not just a fear of catching the disease but a perhaps greater fear of being associated with the disease. And it is this fear, I suggest, that has made the church slow to respond, half-hearted in its pronouncements on the need to care for those with AIDS, and quite unwilling to direct its many resources of people, skills, buildings and money to the benefit of those with AIDS, Why?

There is a belief that if the Christian church gets involved with AIDS it will somehow sully its reputation. But one has to ask: in whose eyes? Those of society? The church is not called to justify itself to society but to Christ its Cornerstone, and he was no stranger to scandal. Before he was even born, his foetus was a cause of scandal. 'Being a man of principle, and at the same time wanting to save her from exposure, Joseph desired to have the marriage contract set aside quietly' (Matt. 1.19). Every word our Lord uttered from his scandalous birth to his even more scandalous death was a cause of scandal.

At the beginning of his ministry he walked into his local synagogue and told his neighbours that he, their carpenter's son, the boy next door, was in himself the fulfilment of prophecy. They were so scandalized they threw him out of town and even tried to kill him (Luke 4.14–30).

He proclaimed forgiveness – scandalous. He befriended the outcast – scandalous. He told a story in praise of the despised Samaritans – scandalous. He healed on the sabbath – scandalous.

But of all his actions, surely his death upon the cross was the most scandalous of all, equalled only by the claims of his followers that God had raised to life the one whom men had sentenced to death. A common criminal is the Son of God, a man condemned and shunned shall come again and judge the earth.

As God in his wisdom ordained, the world failed to find him by its wisdom, and he chose to save those who have faith by the folly of the Gospel. Jews call for miracles, Greeks look for wisdom; but we proclaim Christ – yes, Christ nailed to the cross; and though this is a stumbling-block to Jews and folly to Greeks, yet to those who have heard his call, Jews and Greeks alike, he is the power of God and the wisdom of God. (I Cor. 1.21–24).

The Christian church was born in scandal, saved by scandal, commanded always to follow a path which those who do not know its Lord will always see as scandalous.

So the fear of becoming involved which the church – both clergy and laity – have so far evinced, is the result of a human fear of causing scandal, of upsetting people, of risking its respectable image, of becoming 'one of them' instead of 'one of us'. But Christ let himself be regarded as 'one of them', as an outcast. He was not afraid of scandal, only concerned with the effect of being ostracized on the self-worth of those who were outcast. He risked scandal and death to show that those whom society condemns and ostracizes are not so rejected by God.

If the first of our fears is of contagion – social or medical – the second is closely allied to it. It is fear that makes us want to separate ourselves from the disease by denying it, by pretending AIDS could never affect us. We deny it in order to protect ourselves from it. We are forced by this denial to also deny reality to the people already suffering from the disease. We convince ourselves that they do not concern us. We jump to the conclusion that those who have 'caught' the disease also 'caused' the disease. We see them as responsible for their situation and so relieve ourselves of responsibility to care from them. They are no longer our brothers, so we are no longer their keepers.

We lump them together into groups. We refer to them not as people but as numbers, not as suffering human beings but as victims. We label them and thereby distance them. We separate humanity into sheep and goats and make it clear that we are the sheep and we belong inside a fold in which there is no room for them.

One result of our segregational approach is that even now people in the West choose to be ignorant of the global nature of the problem and so fail to make available the resources that would reduce the scale of this tragedy in the developing countries.

Because we will not 'own' the sick in our national family, we cannot recognize the sick in our global family. It is 'every man for himself' and the 'survival of the fittest'. The concrete jungle has become a moral jungle.

One example of this denial of the closeness of AIDS and of the claims on us of people with AIDS is our absurd labelling of high-risk groups of people. This is totally without medical foundation. The risk of being exposed to the virus which can cause AIDS lies in types of activity not in types of people. To prevent the sexual transmission of AIDS, we have all to stop having unprotected penetrative inter-course, whether vaginal or anal, heterosexual or homosexual.

Another example of this desire to separate ourselves from people with AIDS is the often-heard call for mass-screening. The fact that it is utterly impractical and would be ruinously expensive to test everyone, does not stop us wanting everyone tested – that is, everyone else, for of course, we are not at risk! The fact that everyone would need to be tested again and again several times a year, still does not make us realize that such testing would merely fuel the panic we were trying to assuage.

So it is not the facts about AIDS that should alarm us, nor even how little we know about AIDS. What is really terrifying is our unwillingness to face those facts – even when they could comfort us – and our inability to live with the incompleteness of our knowledge about AIDS. We want clear simple answers and we want them now. And because no one can give us what we want, we invent the answers we want to hear.

We invent groups of people whom we perceive to be at risk. We invent schemes to identify these people. We make plans to segregate them, so we can distance ourselves from them. We create labels and others ways of using language to help us deny our shared humanity and our shared suffering. We replace brother with deviant, sister with black, keeper with warder.

But even so, our fear of contagion and our denial of involvement are not causes but symptoms, symptoms of a dis-ease which goes deeper even than our need for a scapegoat to fuel our racial and sexual exclusivities.

What the reaction of people in the West to AIDS really shows is that we have not yet come to terms with those Siamese twin taboos: sex and death. We are not yet at ease in our sexuality, not yet ready to face our mortality, not yet aware of any link between them. It is as if two live wires have been exposed and when these are linked the resulting shock frightens us to death.

But these issues, vital though they are for our healing as human beings, are not to do with AIDS. AIDS is a viral not a moral problem, an issue of health, not of sexual morality. It is only because the AIDS virus can be transmitted sexually and then can develop into AIDS in some people and for these people can result in death, that these taboos have any link with AIDS at all.

The trouble with so much Christian writing and thinking so far on AIDS is that it assumes this link and uses AIDS as an opportunity to reassert traditional Christian sexual morality. People with AIDS deserve better from us than that we should wield AIDS as a big stick in a sermon on chastity.

The true curse of AIDS lies in our lovelessness, a lovelessness that desires to deny the disease and to separate ourselves from those who have the disease. It is a lovelessness that makes us want to point the finger of blame for the disease on those who have the disease and to dehumanize and ostracize them to the extent of denying our common humanity with them. It is a lovelessness that makes us wilfully blind to our membership of one global family and to the suffering in that family. It is a lovelessness that results from our failure to come to terms with our mortality and our sexuality – in a word, with our humanity. Because it is lovelessness, it has excluded God.

It is only by acknowledging and confessing this to him, knowing that our repentance will meet with his forgiveness, that we shall have lifted from our shoulders the intolerable and distorting weight of a curse we have brought upon ourselves.

AIDS and the God of love

We know that God has a will for us in the face of AIDS, but we do not as yet know what that will is because we do not know where he is. In the search for any missing person, it is sensible to start with a picture, so let's see if we can build up a picture of him.

We know he is a God of justice, but his view of justice is quite different from ours. For us, justice could be described as the upholding of right in a way that is seen to be fair. But God's justice is blatantly unfair. He favours the younger brother who cheats his way into the family inheritance over the honourable older brother. He pays the same wages to the latecomer as to the worker who has been hard at it all day. He kills a fatted calf for a young ne'er-do-well, but never thinks to give a pat on the back to the son who stayed home and kept to the straight and narrow.

For us, justice is maintained by the discovery and punishment of vice. Yet when we are convicted, God pays the price of our freedom. If we are sent to jail – even for crimes on God's statute book – he has told his followers to come and visit us, thereby assuring us of his continuing love and concern for us. If we are sentenced to death for our crimes, it is his Son who dies alongside us.

And God displays this inequity not only in the way he treats all those who have broken his laws, but in deliberately flouting that most cherished judicial ideal: impartiality. God is very partial. He has pet hates. He points the finger at the respectable and the righteous and accuses them of smug self-interest and pride. He points the finger at those who are rich and powerful and accuses them of selfishly wielding their power.

God has favourites. Through his prophets, he promises justice not for everyone but for the downtrodden, for the needy, for the powerless, for the outsider.

Worst of all, the scales of God's justice are fixed. God's justice is loaded with mercy in favour of the disadvantaged, whether or not they (or we) feel they somehow deserve to be disadvantaged.

We can therefore expect that God has not distanced himself from those with AIDS, but has actually taken their side.

Perhaps he has gone further. Perhaps he has picked out people with AIDS and those who care for them for a special blessing. Just as he picked an old man and his barren wife to be the bearers of blessing to every family in the world, just as he picked an insignificant young woman to be the bearer of the One who brings salvation to every family in the world, so now perhaps he is picking those who are outcast to be the means of bringing us all back together, picking those whom we have excluded to be the means of bringing us all home.

This would certainly accord with his past behaviour. In picking Moses to be his spokesman, he chose someone who just could not speak in public (Ex. 4.10). In picking Moses to lead the Israelites, he chose the one man most unacceptable to the Israelites (Ex. 2.14). Of all the people suffering with leprosy, God let it be Naaman who was healed – Naaman who was the commander of the enemy army and who presumably did not even believe in the God of Israel until after he had been healed (II Kings 5.1–19). And when drought hit Israel, God sent his prophet not to a wealthy Israelite for food and shelter but to a Phoenician widow and her son, themselves on the point of starvation (I Kings 17.8–16).

It is noteworthy that Jesus himself drew attention to these last two examples in his first public proclamation (Luke 4.25–30). His purpose is clear. It is not just to show solidarity with those whom we consider unworthy of human society let alone divine favour, but to show the power of God's might.

As he passed by, he saw a man blind from his birth. And his

21

disciples asked him, 'Rabbi, who sinned, this man or his parents, that he was born blind?' Jesus answered. 'It was not that this man sinned, or his parents, but that the works of God might be made manifest in him' (John 9.1–3).

Even this superficial sketch of God has led us to expect that we shall find him not among those condemning but among those suffering. He will be with them not because they deserve it but precisely because the rest of us do not think they should deserve any special favours. He is with them in their suffering not only to bring them comfort but also to work in them. This work will reveal his unconditional love, his infinite mercy, his healing power and his eternal blessing.

We can be confident of this because even if we do not know God very well, we do know his Son. Like his Father, the Son shows a preference for the poor, the sick, and the outcast simply because they know their unworthiness, they know they are sinners.

Jesus' life shows this. His star was followed by foreigners, not God's chosen people. Worse, they were not even foreigners who believed in him. They believed truth lay in the stars. Yet they were able to recognize in a peasant's baby, born in a common stable, one who would change the world. The response of these foreign pagans was to worship him. The response of the Jewish leaders was to try to kill him.

His ministry was one of healing. The message he proclaimed was intended to heal the rift between God and his people, between one human being and another, between people and the rest of creation. His miraculous healing of certain individuals reflected the healing nature of his ministry.

He had come to proclaim humanity as mortally wounded. He had come to bring new life to the dying and to offer his own life blood to bring to the peoples of all nations and of all generations the possibility of wholeness, restored unity and health.

He healed them of whatever they lacked for wholeness and of whatever separated them from the society to which they belonged. Whether it was a withered arm or a withered mind or a withered soul, he healed them. He healed them regardless of their sex, age, nationality or status. He healed them regardless of whether they would use that healing and restoration well, or even be grateful to

God for their healing (Luke 17.11–19). He was able to heal them because they acknowledged their need of healing.

The effect of their healing revealed the purpose of that healing. It restored the leper to society, the dead child to its parents, the slave to his master, the paralysed man to his body, the demonic to his right mind.

But time and again the words of healing are words of forgiveness. Jesus did not mean that the paralysed man was paralysed by sin. Rather, Jesus recognized that what was holding that man back from wholeness was not merely a sense of being apart from his body but apart from his God. Jesus' words simultaneously restored him to God and to himself.

So the purpose of Jesus' healing is to restore fullness of life, at-one-ness between the individual who knows his need of healing and his true being, at-one-ness between that restored human being and his community, and at-one-ness between that individual and his God.

In the light of that understanding of the healing purpose of Christ's ministry, it is worth looking more closely at two particular healings: the healing of a leper (because so often people with AIDS are treated like people with leprosy) and the healing of the woman taken in adultery (because so often people with AIDS are attacked for sexual sins).

The healing of a man with leprosy. The passage is Mark 1.40–45. It has parallels in Matt. 8.1–4 and in Luke 5.12–14. It is significant that both Mark and Luke place this healing at the beginning of Jesus' ministry. Matthew places it immediately after the Sermon on the Mount: as Jesus is coming down from the mount, the leper approaches him and Jesus practises what he has just preached.

Luke the physician adds a medical note – the man was 'full of leprosy'. A picture is thereby created in our minds of the most horrifying disfigurement.

All three writers seem to agree that the man risked death to approach Jesus. He came into town, into the crowd. He broke all the rules for an outcast and would have done so only if his need for healing was greater than his fear of losing his life completely.

We can picture the crowd drawing back in horror and revulsion at both the sight and the smell of the disease. The poor man's isolation in the centre of a hostile crowd must have emphasized his apartness from humanity, his sense of having been singled out by God for a terrible punishment, for such was the belief in those days. He was accursed and he knew it.

The reaction of the crowd was only natural when they found themselves face-to-face with a disfiguring and ultimately death-dealing disease which had the curse of God written all over it. It is our reaction too on seeing for the first time the wasted body of a person with AIDS bearing the tell-tale lesions of Kaposi's Sarcoma. We have tried to segregate them, or allowed them to segregate themselves, into ghettoes and hospitals. We have tried to put them out of sight and so out of mind. We have shunned them. Yet greater is their need than their fear of any further harm we could do to them.

The leper approaches, begging on his knees: 'If you will, you can make me clean.' This is no abject plea. It has dignity. It throws out a challenge: *if* you will. It shows faith. It acknowledges that the power of those who belong to God is the power to heal, to make whole, to restore to communion with God and with humanity.

Then the crowd and the man look to Jesus. So amazed are they by what they see that it has been preserved for us. Jesus is moved to pity. On another occasion we hear of Jesus being 'deeply moved and troubled' (John 11.33). Here, Jesus is moved to pity by the man's overwhelming need.

What Jesus does next would have appalled the crowd as much as the later healing would have delighted them. He reaches out and touches the man. What matters is that he touches him before he heals him. He touches him with the marks of the disease still on him. He accepts him as he is and restores him to community with a touch. He does this knowing that the law makes clear that anyone who touches an untouchable becomes an untouchable.

So what Jesus is doing is not just to show pity or even acceptance. He is sharing that man's outcast state. He is coming alongside him in his suffering and rejection and making himself publicly 'one of them'.

Then, picking up the man's own phrase, he says, 'I will; be clean.' The physical cure follows, but the real healing has already been achieved.

The pattern of Jesus' ministry has therefore much to teach us about proclaiming the need we all have of God's healing touch. But that proclamation leads immediately to a challenge for us to follow him and help him bring healing to our world.

We are called to be his instruments in restoring our world to wholeness. We do this by going out from the security of our homes and families and by making ourselves known and available to those in need. We do not force what we have to offer upon them, but when they approach us, we reach out and touch them. We accept them as they are. We share their isolation and suffering – and if need be we share their outcast state. We do not hold back our compassion or our company. We risk contagion. We risk being shunned by our families, friends and neighbours. We touch the untouchable and thereby allow our touch to be an instrument of God's healing.

It is only when we embrace those actually dying of AIDS that the miracle happens. Father Michael Lopes, OP, the Co-ordinator of the AIDS ministry in the archdiocese of San Francisco, described it thus after he had been to visit a young man in an AIDS ward:

> 'After I had given him the sacraments, he lifted himself up from the bed and I gave him the Kiss of Peace. I held him in my arms and ran my hand down his back. I could feel all these lesions on his back and it was a moment of great pain for me. It became very evident to me at that moment that I was holding the Body of Christ. Then, I knew what Our Lady felt when she took the Lord's body from the cross.'
>
> (quoted by Timothy Radcliffe OP in *AIDS: Meeting the Community Challenge* ed. Vicky Cosstick, St Paul Publications 1987, p. 116)

From what we know of the nature of God, we had expected to find him on the side of people with AIDS, bringing mercy and blessing. From what we know of his son, we find him in people with AIDS, making whole and restoring what was broken and discarded.

It is in the light of this revelation that the prophecy contained in Isaiah 53 takes on its full meaning. Christ's offering of himself for sin involves his taking into his own body the ugliness (v. 2), grief and sorrow (v. 3) of the suffering world to such an extent that we turn away from him in revulsion (v. 3b) and think him accursed (v. 4). But the truth is that this total identification of himself with the outcast and the diseased in us all is God's will (v. 5 & 10). 'Because he poured out his soul to death, and was numbered with the transgressors; yet he bore the sin of many, and made intercession for the transgressor (Isa. 53.12b), joy, peace and the free offer of mercy can go out to all of us. This wonderful news is celebrated by creation. But Isa. 35 tells us it is not the rich fields and teaming rivers which celebrate but the wilderness, dry land and desert that rejoice. Among humanity it is not the young, the beautiful and the strong who celebrate but the lame who dance and the dumb who sing for joy.

Although all creation enjoys the benefit his sacrifice has bought, it is only a blessed remnant, who realize they are the 'ransomed of the Lord', who celebrate the new fullness of life in harmony with the despised and the rejected. It is they who

shall return,
and come to Zion singing;
everlasting joy shall be upon their heads;
they shall obtain joy with gladness,
and sorrow and sighing shall flee away

(Isa. 35.10).

This is why those who would be greatest should regard themselves as of least account and servants to all, because the Lord has placed at the head table of his great banquet those who, like Lazarus (Luke 16.19–31), are covered in sores, the poor, the maimed, the blind and the lame, those in the ditches and hedgerows of earthly kingdoms (Luke 14.15–24). If the rest of us are allowed in at all, it will only be as servants to wash their feet (John 13).

So we had better get used to our lowly position now, for our qualification as servants in heaven will depend on our abilities as servants to these, God's chosen, on earth (Matt. 25.31–45).

It should not therefore shock us to discover the face of Christ in a young man with AIDS, because Jesus has always meant what he said and he said that he was the hungry man to whom we gave or refused food; he was the stranger whom we shunned or welcomed; he was the naked one whom we clothed or shamed; he was the convicted prisoner (not 'innocent victim') whom we visited or forgot; and he was the sick person, the person with AIDS, whom we loved or loathed.

Yet still we hesitate. It could be fear of taking that step which translates faith into action, but we persuade ourselves it is something else. We persuade ourselves that it is our human sense of justice which demands there should also be blame and punishment, sin and consequence, cause and effect. Reluctantly we admit that Jesus said:

Judge not and you will not be judged;
condemn not, and you will not be condemned;
forgive, and you will be forgiven;
give, and it shall be given to you;
good measure, pressed down, shaken together,
running over, will be put into your lap.
For the measure you give
will be the measure you get back

(Luke 6.37, 38).

This makes us feel guilty at condemning people ourselves, so we make them out to be enemies of God. People with AIDS, we say, have offended God and so deserve to be punished.

Perhaps this was why Jesus included in his list people like prisoners. They are not prisoners of conscience. They are not martyrs to a great cause. They are men and women who have broken God's own commandments not to kill or steal. Yet still Jesus says we should come alongside them.

At the point of his own death as a common criminal, Jesus turned to another common criminal and offered him the unique privilege of entering heaven with Jesus (Luke 23.39–43). That same Christ suffers today beside people with AIDS, showing them the same acceptance and offering them the same promise.

Also in his list of people whom we should serve are the sick. We know that in Jesus' day, certain illnesses were seen to be linked in the same sort of 'sinful-cause/suffering-effect' chain that we sometimes like to think of today. We have already looked at this problem in relation to John 9.1–7, where Jesus was asked for whose sins a man had been born blind.

The same problem is taken up in a different form in Luke 13.1–5. Two catastrophes, possibly connected with Zealot activity, raise the question of whether the people who suffer directly as the result of disasters of any kind are more sinful than the rest of us. Although the particular disaster to which they refer is not clear, Jesus' answer is unambiguous. We are all equally sinful, equally deserving punishment and will all equally perish unless we repent.

So whether we view AIDS from the inside (as a disease affecting me) or from the outside (as a calamity affecting my society), Jesus offers the same answer. We shall all perish unless we repent. But the manner of our present suffering does not reflect any particular individual's sin, rather it reflects the sinful state of human beings. So the fact that I a sinner am suffering now does not mean I am more or less a sinner than anyone else or that this particular suffering is meant by God as a punishment for any particular sin of mine.

AIDS, therefore, is not God's means of punishing particular individuals for their specific sins, but looked at aright, AIDS can serve to remind us of the disordered, misdirected state of humankind. Nor is it the main such indicator.

Our reliance on nuclear warheads and on the threat of destroying this planet in order to secure the sovereignty of our own tiny bit of it, is a clearer picture of the idolatry that characterizes people in the twentieth century. We have placed our trust in our own destructive strength instead of in God.

Another example would be the wilful pollution of our seas and sky; or the way we have wiped out some species of animal, bird and fish life. So AIDS is just one example among many of our refusal to live together in harmony with each other and with nature, and our reaction to AIDS is a condemnation of the way we have misunderstood the nature and will of God.

But there is one more healing at which we must look in detail if we are to understand what methods we should use as we seek to serve the Christ we meet in the person with AIDS.

The healing of a woman taken in adultery. At first sight it may seem extraordinary to speak of healing in relation to a story we are more used to seeing in terms of forgiveness or rescue or warning. Certainly all these elements are contained in the story. The woman is forgiven, she is rescued from those who would otherwise have stoned her to death, and there is a warning in 'Go and sin no more.' But they are part of, and less important than, Jesus' real concern, which is for her healing. The passage is usually in John 7.53–8.11. Other ancient manuscripts omit it, or place it in Luke 21.38ff.

In many ways it repeats the story of the healing of the leper. At the end of his ministry we see Christ reiterating what he was saying and doing at the beginning of his ministry – living out his concern for outcasts in such a way as to bring them back into the community.

The first point to note is that this was no chance meeting: it was set up to trick Jesus. We are told that the scribes and the Pharisees actually brought the woman to him. Presumably they felt that they could rely on his defending her and could use this as evidence against him in court and also use it to destroy the credibility of his teaching with the crowds.

That the woman had been caught in the act of adultery is not in doubt. Indeed, the law demanded there were eye-witnesses to prove her guilt before a sentence of being stoned to death could be imposed.

What perhaps offends our modern sense of justice is that the guilty man is not produced. Perhaps this is why Jesus pauses before commenting: he had only half the situation before him. Since the purpose of his healing ministry is to make whole and to restore to communion, how can this be achieved without the wronged husband and the guilty man also being present? The fact that the crowd then and most readers of the story now do not normally notice this omission is a reflection of the continuing male myopia on the subject of sexual sin: woman is always seen as the seductress and thus as bearing more guilt than the man. For the same reason today prostitutes are arrested and not their clients.

So the woman is being made into a show-case. She alone is picked out and made to stand in the centre of a circle of her accusers. Her isolation, like that of the leper, is complete.

Instead of speaking, Jesus draws in the sand. He is deliberately not looking at her. He feels for her. He senses her mortal embarrassment and he helps her by drawing the attention of the crowd away from her and on to himself. He has identified with her shame and taken it on to himself.

The accusers find the silence unbearable. They press Jesus to answer, convinced they have him cornered. Jesus, we are told, sits up straight. The tension mounts. The crowd knows that in his teaching on sexual morality Jesus has upheld the Jewish belief in fidelity and in the sanctity of marriage and has even gone further and warned of the adultery of the mind. Surely now he will not go back on his word?

But Jesus' reply, when it comes, is not a statement but a question, not a condemnation but an invitation. He invites anyone present who feels himself to be without sin to cast the first stone.

There is silence, awkwardness, as the embarrassment shifts from the woman to the crowd. One by one they slink away.

Jesus has in effect reminded them of another of his teachings, namely that it is not for human beings to judge or condemn one another.

Even when they are at last alone together, Jesus – who is without sin and alone qualified to cast that stone – does not condemn her. The whole episode has been an example of how Jesus wants the laws of God to be seen and applied. They are there to help us stay in communion with God and with each other. But when the laws of God are broken and the oneness of that relationship is broken, God wants only to heal that rift before we end up cutting ourselves off from him completely. It is not he who is doing the 'cutting off', but we who are doing it to ourselves. God will not even allow our breaking his laws to cut us off from him. As St Paul pointed out, nothing can separate us from the love of God which is in Christ Jesus (Rom. 8.31–39).

This is why we are not permitted to judge or condemn one another, even on the most blatant evidence: because the act of doing so encourages us to think that we are morally superior, that we are without sin. We have neither the human right nor the divine permission to say that someone with AIDS has become infected as a punishment for their own sexual sin.

To those of us who are guilty of sexual sin Christ says 'Go and sin no more'. But he says it quietly, when we are alone with him.

This is no encouragement to sin (Rom. 6.1–4). Rather it is a reminder that we are all sinners, all deserving punishment, but that God's will for us is his free gift to us: that we should be justified by his grace as a gift (Rom. 3.21–26).

All this has shown us that the accursed are those who have cut themselves off from God and that the blessed are those who have seen their need of healing and accepted this healing as a free gift from God which then restores us to union and fellowship with him and with one another.

The time has come to try and draw all these strands together. We have seen that the curse of AIDS is our own lovelessness; that those who have become infected with AIDS are not responsible for causing the disease; that the attitude of God to what we see as the particular sexual sins of certain individuals is that we are all sinners, all alike deserving punishment.

But AIDS is not God's punishment on them or on us. God does not want to punish us. He sent his Son to offer and to achieve for us that true healing which restores us to wholeness with ourselves, fellowship with each other and communion with him. Christ is in people with AIDS, sharing their suffering and their isolation. He bids us follow him and he bids us serve him by serving those with AIDS. As we do so, we discover it is the Body of Christ himself we are visiting, bathing, embracing.

If humanity has turned AIDS into a curse, Christians can turn it into a blessing by proclaiming AIDS not as sin but as symptom of the disordered and misdirected lives – the idolatry – of our generation. When we acknowledge our need of him, repent those occasions on which we have refused his comfort and help to others and to ourselves, we clear the way to seeing the real nature of healing.

But God can only offer blessing – we have to accept it. If we allow our service and love to people with AIDS to be one means through which God's healing love reaches those who are physically ill, we shall find that we too are being healed of whatever holds us back from full fellowship with him.

I am called to be Christ to my brother and sister with AIDS as they are Christ to me. I am called to be the means through which my brother and sister with AIDS are offered healing for their deep moral fracture as they are called to offer the same healing to me. It is as we serve each other, help to heal and re-create each other that we shall find in AIDS not a curse but a true source of blessing.

Material for prayer and reflection

Whilst this material is intended for group use, some individuals may find it helpful if they are working through the book on their own.

What can we say about AIDS?

In view of the fact that so many people still feel AIDS does not concern them and that people with AIDS have brought it on themselves, this summary of a positive Christian response to AIDS may help you marshal your arguments when you try to persuade your fellow Christians to rethink their attitudes and to challenge them to join you in showing God's love to people with AIDS.

God

Ours is a creative not a destructive God (Gen. 1,2) who, even knowing our propensity to evil, chooses to bind himself to us in a covenant of acceptance and mercy (Gen. 8.20–22). He offers us blessing not curse (Gen. 12.1–3) and invites us into a relationship of love with him and with each other (Luke 10.25–28). He sends to us his only son to show us that not even death can separate us from his love (Rom. 8.31–39) for he came to bring us not death but life in all its fullness (John 3.16,17).

AIDS

AIDS is a viral not a moral condition. It does not discriminate on grounds of age, gender, race or sexual orientation and nor should we. That we have chosen to see it as a curse from God is a reflection on us not on him. In panic, we have projected on to AIDS our disease at our sexuality, mortality and our fear of contagion. To distance these unresolved terrors we have scapegoated blacks and gays. Thus the true curse of AIDS is our own lovelessness. Yet AIDS could be a God-given opportunity to address and resolve these issues and to acknowledge our mutual need of repentance, forgiveness and healing. AIDS is not sin but symptom of a disordered society and diseased psyche.

Christ

Christ was not afraid of being associated with society's outcasts. Rather he chose to associate with them (Matt. 8.10–13) and promised them places of honour in his kingdom (Luke 16.19–31; Luke 14.15–24). Christ was not afraid of contagion: in the presence of disfiguring disease he 'reached out and touched' even before he healed the leper (Mark 1.40–45; Luke 5.12–15). His was a healing ministry (Luke 5.31,32), the function of which was to restore those who acknowledged their need of healing to community with God and with each other. Jesus taught specifically that disease and disaster are not punishment for specific individual sin (John 9.1–3; Luke 13.1–5) and that we must never presume to judge or condemn others (Matt. 7.1–5; Luke 6.37,38) because, especially in respect of sexual sin, we are in no position to throw stones (John 7.53–8.11).

Us

We are called to follow him, knowing that as we serve the sick we are literally tending him (Matt. 25.31–46), such is his identification with those whom society would ostracize. As he suffered crucifixion beside a man who felt himself to have been justly condemned to death and promised him the first place in Paradise (Luke 23.32–43), so Christ today totally shares the suffering of those with AIDS whom the world rejects, in order that no one should die in ignorance of the knowledge that God loves them. As we minister to people with AIDS, they minister to us. Together we help to re-create each other and receive the blessing of his healing.

Recommended reading

AIDS and the Church (Church and Society Documents), World Council of Churches, March 1987.

What can we pray about AIDS?

Depending on how you see God at work in AIDS, one of these prayers may be helpful:

O Almighty God, who in thy wrath didst send a plague upon thine own people in the wilderness, for their obstinate rebellion against Moses and Aaron: and also, in the time of King David, didst slay with the plague of Pestilence threescore and ten thousand, and yet remembering thy mercy didst save the rest: Have pity upon us miserable sinners, who now are visited with great sickness and mortality: that like as thou didst then accept of an atonement, and didst command the destroying Angel to cease from punishing, so it may now please thee to withdraw from us this plague and grievous sickness: through Jesus Christ our Lord. Amen.

from The Book of Common Prayer

Lord,
You created us in love for love.
We have betrayed that love in hate and fear of those you made our brothers and sisters.
Forgive our lack of love.

Your nature is always to show mercy
Yet we your church have not been merciful to those who most need mercy.
Forgive our lack of love.

You came in Christ Jesus to call sinners
Yet we have excluded them from your forgiveness, forgetting our own sin.
Forgive our lack of love.

Your will is to bring us blessing
Yet we have wrongly proclaimed your curse.
Forgive our lack of love.

You have poured on us abundance of all good things and the knowledge of all good things.
Yet we have not shared our skills and our resources with those of our sisters and brothers poorer in some ways than us.
Forgive our lack of love.

The cries of your suffering children rise continually to you
Yet we have hardened our hearts to ignore them.
Forgive our lack of love.

In all our ways we shown ourselves unworthy by our lovelessness to be called your children
Yet we need your love and our lives depend upon your mercy.
Forgive us, heal us, restore us.

Help us to seek the forgiveness of those who have been cast out by our rejection, wounded by our cruelly careless words, scorned by our self-interest. Help us to devote ourselves to those who live with HIV and AIDS so that with them we may seek and find the healing our world needs.
Amen.

PART TWO

Loving Ourselves

Loving Ourselves

Introduction

This part of the book assumes that your theology of AIDS is that God is our loving mother and father who cares even more tenderly for those of his children suffering rejection, alienation, fear and pain and that he is calling us to serve him in our brothers and sisters with HIV infection and illness for our mutual healing.

It suggests that all we have to bring to this work is ourselves: our preparedness to come alongside anyone who is hurting, to share their pain, to offer them our love in his name and together to seek new meaning and purpose in life. In other words, to love our neighbours as ourselves.

This implies that we should love ourselves. There is a proper self-love which characterizes all those who find themselves accepted by people living with any potentially life-threatening illness. Such people know who they are and are comfortable with who they are. They know their weakness and manage to stay vulnerable; they know their feelings and their own need for support; they know their fears and are at ease with their own sexuality and their own mortality.

The aim of Part Two is therefore to help us recognize and begin to address what holds us back from this proper self-love. It is necessary we start this process before we meet people who are HIV+ because AIDS will bring us up against aspects of our society and of ourselves which we shall find shocking and distressing. If we are not to shock and distress others we need to have worked through in advance how we feel about disease, about the many expressions of human sexuality, about our own dying and about the cutting short of life, about contagion and closeness and about the anger, loss and despair – often directed against God – which people who are dying may feel.

In the final stages of this illness people with AIDS may be aware of little else but how appalling they look and feel. They may not just be skin and bones but putrefying, disfigured skin and bones. They may be blind or deaf or at times demented, but this might make them even more conscious of how repulsive they feel. If you go into their sick room and show you can't cope, that you cannot still recognize, accept and love them, how on earth will they be able to believe themselves known and loved by God?

Perhaps they have had a friend die like this and now face their own diagnosis. Their only thought is suicide: they don't want to live to face a death like that. If you have not already worked through your own feelings on suffering and suicide, they may not be prepared to wait around until you do.

So for their sakes as much as for our own, because we need healing as much as they do, we must face up to how we feel about those issues which are certain to be raised by our contact with people affected by AIDS. We shall attempt to do this by looking at ourselves under three headings: loving our weakness, our feelings and our fears. The work is painful but essential for until and unless we can learn to know, accept, forgive and cherish ourselves, we cannot learn to love others as we love ourselves.

Loving our weakness

Our weakness in the face of AIDS may at first appear to be our fear of it, but when we look deeper, it is actually our ignorance. We need to know the medical facts about AIDS to put our own fears of contagion into perspective, to learn to express our love appropriately, and to inform our understanding of what people who are HIV+ are facing or going through. Thus our weakness can be described as an under-developed muscle which needs strengthening with exercise. Too much exercise, too much medical knowledge and it hardens us into experts. Just enough knowledge and we can control our unreasonable fears yet stay vulnerable to feeling and therefore able to share the fears and feelings of others.

I want you to imagine that for some time you have been feeling run-down. Your GP sends you to the hospital for a blood-test. You notice the young doctor seems rather harassed, depressed and overworked, and you feel a bit of a fraud for wasting his time, but after a few rather strange questions, a sample of your blood is taken and you are told to come back in a fortnight.

You do so. The same doctor is on duty. In fact, he looks as though he hasn't been off-duty since you last saw him. The results are through, he says, and your mind prepares itself for news that you are slightly anaemic or have picked up an exotic virus which will make a delightful conversation starter at parties.

Yes, he says, you have a virus. The virus that causes AIDS. You can't believe it. There must have been a mix-up. You've got someone else's results. It can't be you. You're not like that. You lose your temper. He loses his. He tells you it serves you right: 'If you will lead that sort of life-style, what do you expect? You get what you deserve.'

How do you feel? How will you feel at that party tonight at which, because your friends know you have been for a blood-test, they'll ask you for the result? How will you tell your family? Your partner? Your children? Your neighbours? Your boss? Your minister or priest?

'How did you get on?'

'I've got AIDS. Would you pass the salt? Thank you.'

Jot down your initial reactions. Pause for a moment. Then read on.

The diagnosis is so unthinkable that you've probably already missed the point. The blood-test you have taken cannot reveal AIDS. It can only reveal antibodies to the virus that can cause AIDS. This is not prevarication. There is a very real difference.

It wasn't weakness that led you to jump from a positive antibody result to full-blown AIDS, but ignorance. So the first thing you need is to find out the facts.

The facts about AIDS

The first fact about AIDS is that the facts given here are out-of-date. This is inevitable. Although AIDS may have been around for a long time, it has only recently been recognized by medical research. A lot of time and money is suddenly being spent on it so discoveries appear to come out thick and fast. But medical experience of the disease is very recent so, for example, news of a 'cure' should be regarded with caution since there hasn't been time to know how effective such a 'cure' is, nor what the long-term effects of it are.

Statistics on AIDS are even less reliable. Some countries don't like to admit that they have a problem with AIDS, perhaps because it might affect their international image. Others do not have the means to collate the figures, perhaps because all their available resources are already overstretched dealing with the problem.

Facts and figures are anyway not of paramount importance. AIDS does not exist in an academic vacuum but in people. People's attitudes and expectations with regard to AIDS are equally as important as what AIDS is or could be doing to their bodies. People with AIDS are living longer now not simply because of better treatment but because of their own healthier attitudes towards AIDS.

Bearing in mind the partiality of our knowledge and the partiality of its usefulness, what do we know about AIDS?

AIDS is caused by a virus. A virus is the smallest of all disease-producing organisms. Viruses, for example, cause the common cold and influenza. Since medical research has made no progress in combating these viruses, we should not be over-optimistic at their chances of quickly curing AIDS.

The AIDS virus attacks the body's T-cells. These are the cells which the body uses to fight disease. They form part of the body's defence system. When the body's defence system becomes aware of the presence of a potentially harmful virus, it reacts by developing antibodies to neutralize or destroy it. It is these antibodies which are detected by the so-called AIDS test. All that test can tell us is that at some point in the past this person has come into contact with another person carrying the virus and has acquired the virus from them. They have *A*cquired a virus to which the body's *I*mmune *D*efence system has begun to react. If at some future point that person goes on to display certain symptoms which have been identified as associated with this disease, then a *S*yndrome is diagnosed. Hence the words AIDS means *A*cquired *I*mmune *D*eficiency *S*yndrome.

But we do not know enough to say that the virus which can cause AIDS always and inevitably does cause AIDS. This virus, which used to be called HTLVIII, is now universally called HIV – Human Immunodeficiency Virus.

Nor is it possible to say how long ago the HIV virus entered that person's body because the virus lies dormant and may remain undetected for many years. But what is certain is that once inside the body, the virus never leaves it. It is therefore called a retrovirus – it allows opportunistic infections to get into the body because the immune system has been impaired.

A person whose body has already begun to fight off the potentially damaging presence of the HIV virus can look and feel perfectly well. They may therefore be totally unaware of the presence of the virus. This is why all of us have to be careful to protect ourselves and those whom we love, especially by not exchanging body fluids because the virus lives in those fluids, especially in blood.

The virus uses the genetic reproductive mechanism within human cells to reproduce itself. Disguising itself as something harmless, it first confuses and then destroys the T-cells, preventing them from defending the body against all sorts of diseases which a healthy body would have no trouble neutralizing.

These diseases are called opportunistic infections because they can only establish themselves in a person whose immune defence system is not working properly. Once certain recognized opportunistic infections have manifested themselves, the person may be diagnosed as having AIDS, but AIDS is a misleading term because it sounds as if there is only one such disease with a given set of symptoms.

It might help to think of the body as a suitcase. AIDS is like the rust which stops the lock operating and thereby leaves the suitcase vulnerable. I am grateful to the Revd. Carolyn Henson for the description of AIDS as a 'vulnerable state of being' rather than 'having something' or 'carrying something'.

When we speak of people dying of AIDS we are again misleading ourselves because people actually die of other diseases to which they have become susceptible because their immune defence system is not working. AIDS explains why they became susceptible to these other diseases. It is not itself the primary cause of death. These other diseases include various cancers, pneumonias and fungal infections.

Pneumocystis Carinii Pneumonia (PCP). Death results from collapsed lungs and respiratory failure.

Kaposi's Sarcoma (KS). A skin cancer that can be lethal if it invades the lower intestine, lungs or bones.

Cryptosporidosis. A parasite which causes catastrophic diarrhoea and can kill people through dehydration and loss of body salts.

Candidiasis (Thrush). This causes a fungal growth which can block the throat and invade the intestinal tract or the lungs.

There are also various conditions affecting the brain such as *Cytomegalovirus, Cryptococcus neoformans* and AIDS dementia.

If you have the virus and go on to develop AIDS you will die. But not everyone who has the virus does develop AIDS so far as we know at this point in time. Some may develop one or more of these opportunistic infections and then recover and return to good health. Others may develop one of a complex of diseases associated with people with HIV infection (ARC) and then go back to good health. ARC stands for Aids-Related Complex.

In different parts of the world ARC is defined differently. Cryptosporidosis or PCP – on their own – may lead doctors to diagnose people as having ARC rather than AIDS. Someone who has AIDS has a particularly low T-cell count and more than one serious opportunistic infection.

But another word of caution is necessary. Because funds are short and treatments expensive, it has been the experience of some people in this country that they are diagnosed as having AIDS rather than ARC in order for the hospital to get the funds it needs to treat them.

It is much simpler – and both more accurate and more positive – to describe people as either 'well with HIV-infection' or 'ill with HIV-infection' because this is how they experience it.

Those who are infected with the virus but have not gone on to develop AIDS do, however, remain at risk of AIDS dementia because the HIV virus attacks and destroys brain cells as well as T-cells.

But if AIDS is not curable, it is treatable. Each of the opportunistic infections can be treated and often controlled. Because the infection usually returns when the treatment is stopped, scientists are looking for a way of attacking the virus itself. They are beginning to find that drugs like AZT, perhaps used in combination rather than on their own, can stop the virus replicating itself, especially if treatment begins early. However, such treatments cannot yet repair damaged immunity and so may not always be able to prevent people with the virus going on to develop AIDS.

A vaccine is thought by many to be the long-term solution, but it would be very much a long-term answer. It may not be available for another decade, and when it is available, it will be too late to save thousands of lives and, unless we see AIDS as a matter of justice, the cost of the vaccine may be too high for poorer countries which are already the worst affected.

There is now beginning to be recognized a link between poverty and AIDS as between poverty and susceptibility to all disease. In countries where malnutrition and TB are present, HIV infection is more likely to lead quickly to AIDS. Poverty is a matter not for charity but for justice.

Meanwhile the virus continues to infect more people. In any country, in any population, the rate of spread of the virus is very similar. For each case of AIDS there are estimated to be at least 100 people with HIV. Because people with HIV may be displaying no symptoms, they may be unaware of the risk to themselves and to those with whom they have close contact.

Yet the virus is very difficult to acquire. The two main routes of transmission are blood and other body fluids. Mothers can pass on the virus to their babies either in the womb or through the breast, but some research dismisses breast-feeding as a likely cause.

Blood. In wealthier countries screening of all blood supplies has removed almost all danger from blood transfusions, but nearly half of British haemophiliacs are already infected, according to some reports. But in poorer countries, where blood-screening cannot be afforded and where needles have to be used more than once, often without proper sterilization, this remains a significant route of transmission.

Body fluids. Unprotected penetrative sexual intercourse between an infected and a non-infected person, of either sex, is the most likely method of transmitting the virus which can cause AIDS. Although in America and some parts of Europe some homosexual men were the first identifiable group to become infected, this is not true of the world picture and is anyway changing as more and more heterosexual people become infected.

But even while unprotected vaginal or anal sexual intercourse is the most likely route of transmission, we cannot say for sure how, in any individual case, it was acquired; whether it was passed on to anyone else, whether, when or if it will develop in that person into AIDS; and whether a cure will be developed in time to help that individual.

This is why it is important we realize how little we know and how uncertain is even what we think we do know. So understanding the facts of AIDS will not prevent or even allay our fears. It can only put them in perspective.

What isn't risky? Fortunately we are much more certain of how HIV infection can *not* be contracted and this is particularly important for those of us who will be caring for people with HIV or AIDS.

You cannot acquire HIV/AIDS through hugging or kissing someone with AIDS. *They need love. They need to be kissed and hugged.*

You cannot acquire HIV/AIDS through eating a meal prepared by someone with AIDS, by sharing cutlery, crockery, towels, sheets or toilets which have been used by someone with AIDS. But you should not share toothbrushes, razors, or anything on to which blood may have spilled. Bleach is enough to destroy the virus if blood drips on to anything. Simply by maintaining good standards of hygiene you will prevent any possible casual risk to yourself or your family. *They need to feel welcome and safe in our homes.*

Although we may be at no risk from them, they are at risk from us. People with AIDS do not need special accommodation in isolation wards. They need and want to be at home with us. They will only need hospitalization for short periods for treatment for an opportunistic infection. But because their bodies' immune system has been weakened, they will be susceptible especially to air-borne diseases in us. What may be mild 'flu for us could prove lethal pneumonia for them, so when we are ill or infectious, we should stay away from them. *They need to be protected from us.*

Because of the popular hysteria over AIDS, people with HIV infection or AIDS are very concerned about confidentiality. They fear that if people know what is wrong with them, they will experience hostility, and that this may lead to them losing their jobs, families and homes. *They need to feel protected by us.*

If someone with AIDS visits you regularly or is a neighbour – *and if they look ill* – what can you say to people if your friend does not want his diagnosis revealed?

Obviously this is something you will need to work out together but it is always best, if only because it is easiest, to be honest. AIDS kills no one. What may be making your friend look and feel ill is cancer or pneumonia, Alzheimer's disease or motor neurone disease. Talk it over with your friend and see if a solution might not be to answer genuine enquirers' concerns by naming the particular opportunistic infection as the cause of the problem.

Again we are seeing that it is less AIDS than our reaction to AIDS that is the real root of the problem as we seek to cope ourselves, and to help others cope, with a diagnosis of HIV infection or ARC or AIDS.

The first weakness we noted in our ability to cope with AIDS was our ignorance of it. Now that has been strengthened through knowledge, a second weakness shows up: how do we live with all this uncertainty?

Let's go back to the imaginary situation of our being told that we are antibody-positive. If the anger and disbelief we experienced ever go away, what are we really left with?

We do not know how we acquired the HIV infection. We do not know if we have passed it on to someone else. We do not know how the infection will affect us. We do not know when or if we shall ever go on to develop AIDS. We do not know anyone else in our situation. We do not know if there will be a cure in time for us. We do not know with whom we dare share this news and our worries about it.

Being antibody positive initially means being in a state of suspended animation. You are caught up on the hooks of so many question marks and no one can offer you any answers at all.

You do not know how your friends and family will react to the news unless you share it with them. If they reject you, how will you cope?

You do not know how your employer – or even your GP – will react. If you tell them – or if they find out – will they befriend you, shun you, refuse to have anything to do with you? What if you lose your job? How will you cope?

Without anything to do all day long and without enough money coming in to pay the bills and the mortgage, how long will you last?

And if, on top of being rejected by family and friends, losing your job and being made homeless, you then go on to develop AIDS, how would you cope? Would you even try? What would coping mean?

Jot down your initial reactions. Pause for a moment. Then read on.

The situations you have been working through are not invented but the real experiences of many people on discovering they have HIV infection or AIDS.

As you can imagine, not having an answer to even the simplest question can bring people to mental illness. Feeling that you have nothing before you but a nightmare of imaginings can bring people to consider suicide. The sheer exhaustion resulting from not being able to drive these thoughts from your mind, and having no one who understands to share them with, can lead people to see themselves as helpless victims, dying of AIDS rather than the same person they always were, now living with AIDS.

Our ability to cope with a situation like this will depend on the range of experiences we have had before and how we have developed skills to cope with them. It will further be affected by our personality, by any previous mental illness, by our motivation, by our faith, by our relationships and by how well those relationships stand up under this new strain.

Our ability to cope will be affected by our financial and work situations, by our neighbours, by our experience of rejection, stigma, harassment or violence. It will depend on our mental and physical state of health. If we are currently feeling fit and healthy, we shall probably find it easier to react positively than if we are already experiencing one of the symptoms of ARC or AIDS when we receive our diagnosis. If we are currently feeling happy with who we are, we are probably going to find it easier to react positively and to feel ourselves in control of AIDS rather than in thrall to AIDS than if we are currently depressed or anxious.

Our ability to cope is largely our ability to have coped in the past and to have devised ways of coping for the future. What chance has an 18-year-old had to develop such strategies? What thought has someone in 'the prime of life' ever given to the imminence of his own death?

Such people will need our help, but we can only help them when we have faced the issues and helped ourselves. We do that by examining our own 'survival muscles', recognizing which ones are weak and need strengthening, and we begin to strengthen them by beginning to flex them in gentle exercise.

Loving our feelings

One way in which we learn to love ourselves is by being honest with ourselves and with each other. For some of us this is most difficult to do in facing up to our feelings. So here are my feelings on visiting someone seriously ill in hospital – it doesn't matter if they have AIDS or another life-threatening illness. As you read it, listen to your own silent reactions. Try to remember which bits rang bells for you and which bits felt alien.

When I visit someone seriously ill in hospital I am terrified. By the time I get to the top flight of stairs, I am breathless, wobbly and my mind is a complete blank.

I have to sit down, rest and face the truth. I am afraid. I think I am afraid of the friend I have come to visit. So I force myself to think about my friend. What my friend means to me. Then I realize I am not afraid of you, my friend. I am really afraid because I feel so powerless to change anything for you.

But you don't want me to change anything, only to be there with you. You expect me to visit you not to cure you. It is I who want to change things, I who want to be your Fairy Godmother and to wave a magic wand to transform your rat-thin body and pumpkin-blotched skin into some enchanted beauty.

I want the power to change things in you to make them easier for me to handle. But I do not have that power and would misuse it if I had it. I have to put away the pretence that I can change anything, and the wish to change anything. I have to accept that, visiting you, I am powerless.

Perhaps that is why I am really afraid. Because I am powerless to change things, I am at your mercy. I am David. You are Goliath. Yet you see it differently. You see yourself as David, so weak you are lying down, so young others are deciding things for you. You see me as Goliath towering over your bed.

That helps to remind me how threatening a visitor is. I must sit, not stand. Sit close and low so our heads are on the same level. So I physically share your sense of being brought low.

That helps me, but still I am afraid. I am in your power, at your disposal and that means that in visiting you I have given you power to affect me. I know that I could come away from your bed a changed person. I don't want to change. I'm not a good person. I know I

49

need to change. But I don't want to change. The more I think about this, the more frightened I become. I become so scared I need something to hold on to, something to reassure me. What comes to mind is a comforting picture of my routine. I plan what I will do after visiting you. I'll go home and shut the door and turn up the fire and make a cup of tea and watch TV and get on with my life. I'll shut you out. I'll shut myself in.

Then I ask myself what you want and I know you wish it was me who had to stay and you who could go home. I remember how, when I was in hospital for what felt to be a long time, I fell into a daydream that I was a sort of nightwatchman taking my turn occupying this hospital bed until the next person in the rota came along to take my place. 'Rather you than me', my friends would say, looking at me trussed up like a pig for slaughter in the steel prison of an orthopaedic bed, my feet in the air and my head on a level with the skirting board. 'No! It's your turn now!', I wanted to say.

So part of my dis-ease at visiting my friend is a guilt that I am healthy and he is not. I have to remind myself that the ill are not guilty and the healthy blameless. If I feel anything, it should be gratitude that I have enough health to visit my friend and he has enough health to enjoy my visit. But I am not there to replace him. I cannot take on his part. I cannot fill in for him. His pain is other than mine.

Thus I realize that I am not only powerless to change his role: I am also powerless to play it for him.

This makes me ask what is my role? I become very aware of how settings bring out the actor in me. Because this is a hospital setting, the play must be drama or tragedy and the theme must be illness or death. The characters in this play will be clearly identified into active and passive roles. The visitor/doctor/nurse is actively doing and the patient is being done to.

I think of Christ's saying: 'Do unto others as you would be done to'. *Do* – active, me a visitor. *Be done to* – passive, my friend the patient.

I realize I have already reduced the potential of this situation to hackneyed melodrama, to unreality. I have already denied the possibility of a totally different scenario. Why can this play not be a farce – the story of how the worm turns on the gardener, the patient turns on the visitor – the anarchy, the upheaval, the role-reversal of farce, or the charm and wonder of seeing life from a different point of view which one gets from the best comedies? Surely this trite melodrama I have written myself into could yet be transformed into what Dante called a Divine Comedy?

So I have to ask myself why I have fallen into the trap of dictating what will happen instead of letting happen whatever does happen? And I have to acknowledge that it's because I'm afraid of the dark – the powerless, vulnerable feeling of being a child again in the long dark night.

To fight my vulnerability, to limit the harm it may do me, I confine the situation. I confine it in time ('I can only stay a little while'). I confine its power to hurt and change me ('I'll play the doctor and you be the patient. It's my game. I make the rules'). Suddenly I realize I have mentally put on the doctor's white coat and the nurse's starched hat, all the protective gear I can find ('I won't take my coat off. I can't stop'). I ask myself why I don't go the whole hog and see if I can borrow a geiger counter from somewhere? I picture myself walking down the ward in a nuclear fallout space-suit . . . and I laugh.

I enjoyed the laugh while it lasted, but now I feel embarrassed. You shouldn't laugh in hospital. Why not? Why should lowered voices and lowered eyes be the accepted way of behaving in hospital? I'm not in church. And who says they're appropriate for church?

So I ask myself how my friend wants to see me. And the answer has to be, smiling. The answer has to be that he wants me at best to make him laugh or at least not to let my mood determine his, my behaviour make him feel he has to be solemn.

So I decide I'll let my smile empower him to set the agenda for this meeting. I acknowledge that my fear is of being changed, of finding our roles reversed.

Then I realize it goes deeper than that. What would happen if our roles were reversed? What if he said 'Good, you're here at last. My shift is over. Your turn on the bed now' – and he got up, put on my health, used my car to make his escape, occupied my home as his hideaway and left me in a hospital bed, stripped of my immunity?

Stripped. Such a powerful word. Made bare. Shown up for who I am. Denuded of power. (That word again.) Put on the receiving end, the sharp end of the needle, punctured by the intruding will of those who are not only dressed, but masked behind uniforms that give them safe, powerful stereo-typed roles to play and leave me a nameless animal in a cage, being experimented on and talked about while I'm still alive, still conscious.

That's why I'm afraid of losing my 'diplomatic' immunity. It's not just a matter of losing the power to do what I feel like and get away with it; not just a matter of losing the safe and respected position in the community which people with diplomatic immunity – and health – enjoy. It's having to endure being subject to rules: to the rule of my illness, to the rule that I'm just one of many patients, nobody special. There are no exceptions for people like me, for patients. We are not special cases. We are not noticed. No one will open the door for me. More importantly, no one will keep that importuning beggar, Death, away from me. No one will go to the door of Death for me, open it, see what it's like and come back and tell me who's there so I can decide whether or not I'm 'at home'. No one will even come with me while I go and answer that knock on my door.

And how am I afraid that I will lose my immunity, my power to comfort and the safety that goes with it? By touching my friend. I am afraid that his touch is a link to my own mortality; that his physical decay is a mirror of my own – that mirror, mirror on the wall, telling me I'm no longer the fairest of them all.

So what I'm afraid of isn't my friend. It's me. I feel ashamed now. But determined. I get up. I go in. I smile. And when I see you, my friend, I wonder what all the fuss was about.

I love you and you've been worried these last ten minutes, wondering where I'd got to. I try to remember what I've learnt. I smile. I embrace you. I sit low beside you, throwing off my coat and with it all the sharp smells of the outside world.

And gently, gently I look into this mirror of my mortality and try to learn to love myself in you. When the time comes to go – a time you choose, not me – and I find myself doing all the things I'd promised to myself as a treat – closing the door, turning up the fire, turning on the kettle and settling down beside the TV – the house seems different. Someone else's. Not somewhere I own anymore. More like visiting a museum. Somewhere that someone I once was once lived.

Stop. Feel it through. Ask how you really feel when you visit someone seriously ill in hospital. Ask what those feelings help you understand about yourself. If you feel ready, share some of these feelings with a group of friends and explore together how we might learn to love ourselves and see ourselves in the people we visit in hospital.

Loving our fears

Part One of this book argued that the reason for the hysteria over AIDS is that we have not yet learnt to come to terms with our Siamese twin fears of our sexuality and our mortality. It would take more than this book to begin to explore those themes adequately, so what appears here must be regarded as the merest introduction to what for most of us will be a life-long quest. But this section will begin to address those fears.

It starts, however, with another fear: the fear that we may not be loved. Like most fears, our awareness of it fluctuates, but when it flaps bat-like round our bed at night, it can express itself like this:

'Does anyone really love me? Perhaps one. Or two. But they only love me because they do not know me. If they knew me like I know me, they would see I don't deserve to be loved. God says he loves me. But he can't really love me. He can only love the good bits of me. The real me is the bad bits. No one can love them. I don't love them myself. In fact, when I weigh 'me' in the scale of good and bad, there's far more bad than good and I'm not sure I love myself. Or even like myself. I like my jokes. But I've heard them all before.

Come to think of it, I've heard everyone's jokes before. They're no better than mine. Some are worse. As people they're no better than me. Some of them are much worse. Even my closest friends have got faults. Big faults. The more I hear about them from other people the more I realize how big my friends' faults are. And the less I like them. I could go off any of them very easily in fact and if I don't think they really love me or know me, I'm damned if I really love them or want to know them.

And if I don't really feel loved by them or by God and I don't think my friends are either, I wonder if there really is any love in the world and what all the fuss is about love.'

There is a Doubting Thomas in all of us, secretly fearing we are not accepted or acceptable, not truly loved or lovable. We have to find a way of holding the feelings expressed in the last passage with the feelings expressed in this one:

'I know I am lovable only if I feel I am loved. I am aware of being lovable only insofar as I am aware of having experienced being loved. Being loved by others has helped me to recognize that God loves me and to see how he expresses his love for me, both directly and through these other people who love me. This pleasant experience of being loved makes me want to love others in a reciprocal way. But in loving others I also begin to experience something of the cost and the pain of love. I am led to recognize that the worst pain is the pain of rejection. Experiencing the power of this emotion I learn its power can both hurt and heal, and so I am led to a deeper experience of how God loves me and what it costs God to love me. With a growing appreciation of the preciousness of all-costly love, I am led closer to him in awe and wonder and begin to want to love him as he loves me. This in turn gives me a feeling of value and teaches me that I am loved, whether or not I am worthy, whether or not I am aware of it or grateful for it: I am loved by him – at least by him – for all that I am and not just for bits of what I am or what I could be. And through that love I am healed.'

There will be an opportunity to reflect further on how we can love our fears of not being loved or lovable at the end of this chapter. But now we move on to look at our fears of those twin spectres, sex and death. Two thousand years of Christian teaching have failed to make us any more comfortable with either our sexuality or our mortality because they have often failed to see either as God-given gifts. What follows is not an attempt to give a definitive Christian answer, even were such a thing possible, but to show that an exposition of these subjects can be positive and yet still truly Christian. Its value may lie in helping you see what you may hitherto unconsciously have believed and by giving you a chance to reassess the validity of those beliefs.

What can we say about sex?

The first thing to say about sex is that it is a gift from God. The fact that we are sexual beings is something to celebrate, to enjoy and to give thanks for.

Like all God's gifts it can be appreciated on many levels: it embraces the balance of male and female elements within each one of us, our individual sexual identity (whether heterosexual, homosexual or, more usually, a mixture of both), the strength of that sexual drive and the means and situations in which we give it expression. It follows from this that we cannot speak of heterosexuality or homosexuality without considering the whole context of human sexuality.

Sex is not just the means of procreation, it is the means of giving and getting intense pleasure, of affirming our affection for an other person and of being affirmed in love. Sex can be separated from 'making children' but it cannot be separated from 'making love'. Sex is one of the most important ways in which we show love and are assured we are loved.

Above all, sex is our God-given opportunity to experience and to share God's creative power. As we know from our other experiences of God, his creativeness goes beyond bringing life to new things, it brings back life to old things. In the same way, making love revitalizes existing relationships and this is just as important as making new human beings. A sexual act which brings about the birth of a child is not a Christian expression of our sexual gift unless it at the same time revitalizes the existing relationship between the parents. So sex in marriage is not always 'right'. Sex can never be 'justified' solely on the basis of procreation. Sex is only 'right' when it is the result of two consenting partners striving to give each other an expression of their love in a way that goes beyond words. Indeed, it may only be a loving act if it is not open to procreation – when, for example, to conceive would be dangerous to the woman or against the probable interests of the child. Sex is not about filling the world with children but filling the world with love. If sex is our God-given opportunity to experience and share his creative power in love, then it follows that our sexuality is our God-given means for experiencing this.

We cannot therefore reject people or regard them as perverted or second-rate on the grounds of their sexuality since we know that our sexuality is not a matter of choice. Indeed, the more we learn about human sexual orientation, the more we are discovering how early in life that orientation is determined. What is already certain is that our sexual orientation is determined before we are of an age to exercise discretion or choice and therefore responsibility. We are not responsible for our sexual orientation: God is. To despise people on the basis of their sexual orientation is to despise what God has given them.

We have further learnt that the ascriptions 'man' and 'woman' are too distinct if they are used to stress our differences, for every one of us contains both male and female hormones, male and female elements. It follows that we are most fully human and most fully what God wants us to be when we recognize and cherish both the male and female within us. It is ludicrous and unChristian to speak of the superiority of one sex over another, or of one sexuality over another.

Furthermore, our sexual orientation gives us grounds to thank God that there is at least one half of the world we can love without wanting to get into bed with them! We may be sexually attracted to the other half of the world but this does not mean we have to have sex with them. We can express love for people who belong to the sex we find attractive without making love to them sexually.

This is the starting point for examining promiscuity, whether heterosexual or homosexual. If we have sex with someone whom we do not really love then we are having substitute sex. We are substituting sex for love, this person for someone we really love, taking pleasure for giving pleasure. We are 'making-do' and this is insulting to the person with whom we are having sex and also insulting to ourselves because it degrades both that person and ourselves. The root cause of promiscuity is not unbridled lust but a low estimation of self and others.

Promiscuity is addictive and like any repeated activity, reinforces and thereby strengthens a pattern of behaviour. In this case it reinforces our low self-esteem and our contempt of other people. Promiscuity is not wrong because it is addictive, it is wrong because it makes more likely that we will ignore and go on repeating our failure to love ourselves, which in turn prevents us loving others.

Promiscuity, however, is dangerous. It is a quest for excitement, for continual proof of our sexual attractiveness to other people gauged by the number of people who will have sex with us rather than by expanding our capacity to love others and be loved by them. Both the unsatisfying nature of these encounters and the sheer tedium of repetition serve to dull the excitement, so we add the spice of danger, of breaking social or legal taboos. The result is the ruin of our health, of our standing in our community and most of all the disabling of our capacity for love. Promiscuity can also be a way of denying our true sexual orientation by seeking anonymous, desperate and intentionally self-degrading means of sexual expression. It's a quest for love and a making-do with lust. It is not the direction of our sexuality which is the problem but our misdirection of it. The cure for promiscuity is not sexual abstension but a learning how to love oneself and value one's sexual orientation so as to learn to love and value others.

The starting point is to acknowledge our sexuality, to recognize and celebrate it as a gift. As with any gift, our choice is still there: it is the choice whether to accept or to reject it. Like any gift from God, if it is rejected it withers and can distort. Rejected, it reduces our range of opportunities to experience God and to express the love which He inspires in us. But if the gift is accepted and embraced, it becomes a blessing because it allows us to feel more acutely our God-intended need for and love of other people. Rejected, it withers and warps our perceptions of ourselves and our relationships with other people. It follows from this that promiscuity and the rejection of one's sexuality are polarized extremes of the same sin.

Sex is a sacrament in potential and its potential is realized when sex is used within the context of a loving relationship as a means of expressing and bringing new life to that relationship. This can happen in marriage but it can also happen outside marriage because the criteria do not depend on how society in general perceives the nature of that relationship, only on how the two people involved see it. Equally, it is possible within a homosexual relationship as well as within a heterosexual relationship, because what matters is the relationship, not the sexual orientation of the partners within that relationship.

To those who would protest that this is not biblical, I would reply that the Bible has nothing to say about homosexuality or homosexuals. Indeed the very word is unknown in the Bible. The Bible condemns homosexual acts, not homosexual propensities, because the writers of the Bible were unaware that people existed who were only attracted sexually to people of the same sex. What the Bible does condemn is homosexual acts by heterosexual people, especially where such acts are offered as worship to other gods. No one today would argue that the Bible was wrong to condemn such idolatrous behaviour.

But what human experience has taught over the centuries and modern science has more recently confirmed, is that homosexual propensity is not a matter of choice for more than ten per cent of the population for some or all of their lives.

This reinforces rather than contradicts the idea that our sexuality is God-given. It is therefore for homosexuals as it is for heterosexuals a means for experiencing his creative power of love. The joy of gay sex is as much a cause for celebration as the joy of heterosexual sex because both joys come from God and both joys bring us closer to God.

Society, under pressure from the church, has decreed that marriage is the proper place for the expression of heterosexual sexuality. Because the church has specifically refused to allow homosexuals to marry, the church cannot dictate the context in which homosexuals express their sexuality. All the church can do is to hold up the heterosexual model of chastity before and fidelity throughout a permanent relationship and ask homosexuals if this model helps them. But the church must also acknowledge the almost insuperable barriers which it has principally been the cause of erecting and which militate against homosexuals achieving any form of permanent relationship. Permanence is difficult for homosexuals because they have been taught by the church to regard themselves as unworthy so their expectations of themselves and of other homosexuals are lowered. The church has created an atmosphere of homophobia in society so that any gay couple setting up home together are likely to meet with hostility at worst and unfair discrimination at best in their attempts to acquire a home, to stay together in that home, and to face the problems of simply living together with another person.

Yet it is through homosexuals that we are learning that our sexuality is not a matter of choice but of gift; that we all contain male and female elements which should be cherished and developed for they can help us to appreciate and enjoy what men and women have in common and thus lead us to celebrate our unity as human beings rather than our apartness as men or women. For to both men and to women has been given, through our sexuality, the means to experience and to share the creative and revitalizing power of God's love.

What can we say about death?

Our feelings and expectations around death are the clearest test of our faith, because faith is confidence of hope based on personal experience and not the confidence of certainty based on inherited knowledge. We do not know what there is after death. Most of us will have only one opportunity to experience death. We shall not be able to take a 'second run at it'.

This is partly why death frightens us: it will prove once and for all not only whether what we have preached was true or just wishful thinking, but also what God thinks about how we have practised what he preached. It is a test of faith and a preparation for judgment.

But even among Christians there is a belief that the only thing in life we can be sure of is death. This is not true. We can always be sure of God. Our sureness of God is that he is. The name God gives himself in the Old Testament is *Jahweh* which means 'I am'. Such a name assures us of more than his existence. It assures of his continuing presence and that implies his continuing concern.

We learn from Jesus to regard God as a Loving Father. The name Jesus gives to God is not 'Father' (with all its sense of distant, foreboding, Victorian paterfamilias) but *Abba*, a child's name for its father. It doesn't translate as 'Dad' (with all its sense of over-familiarity and a relationship we are growing out of or beginning to rely on less) but 'Dada' or 'Daddy'. These are the terms used by the child who is seeking for the first time to put a name to someone he is beginning to recognize as playing an important and cherished part in his life. There is still wonder, a dawning sense of the otherness of the father-figure, a sense of continually-renewed delight in finding himself in the presence of the father-figure. There is no knowledge. Only experience. And that experience is of a loving presence. The experience is direct and personal. This is the true sureness of this life: the ever-present, ever-loving, continuing, concerned presence of God.

His presence is in our birth as well as in our death. It is in the process of our formation in the womb as well as in the process of our disintegration in the tomb. It precedes our birth. It continues after our death. His presence has been with us since before time had any meaning and will continue with us while time loses whatever meaning it has for us now.

God, who has seen me through the trauma of my entry into this world, will surely see me through the trauma of my exit from this world.

Death, therefore, is neither beginning nor end. We do not know what point on the time scale of God's loving presence with us our death occupies. In the vastness of that loving eternity we may even look back on it as not a significant point, certainly not as the most significant point.

But God is not all that we take with us into and beyond death. We shall take ourselves. In the words of Pierre Teilhard de Chardin, in *Le Milieu Divin*, God will 'part the fibres of my being in order to penetrate to the very marrow of my substance and bear me away with (Him)self.' This is how we can answer our fear of the 'aloneness' of death. We shall not be alone. There will be two of us on that journey: God and our essential selves.

But there are other fears that combine to make the thought of death fearful to us. We feel regret for not having spent our time well, guilt for the wrong we have done and for our setting God so lightly aside, fear of deserved punishment, fear of annihilation, fear of rejection, of finding ourselves finally and ultimately unworthy and unloved. We fear the loss of power over others' lives and of control over our own. We fear the loss of attention: that we shall be forgotten by those we love here and ignored or lost in a crowd in the presence of God there.

What these fears show is that when we strip off all the pretence and outward show, we have not learnt to love and value ourselves or God. Yet there is nothing we can learn in death that we can not learn now, nothing we can experience in death that we cannot experience and profit from now. We need to learn to love and value ourselves properly. We begin by acknowledging that we are totally self-centred: we want everyone's attention, we want everyone to think well of us and to bow to our wishes, and at the same time to accept us with all our faults and to love us unreservedly. We know we have not shown unconditional love to others, we have too easily forgotten them and been insensitive to their needs and refused to see that their needs are the same as ours – to be accepted and valued in loving relationships. Therefore we feel we deserve to be punished, because punishment is what we have meted out to those who have displeased us.

We are actually confusing our experience of earthly parents with God as Divine Parent. Yet Jesus went to great pains to correct this misapprehension. The Father he described knew what his children needed before they asked; promised them good things not bad – bread not serpents; promised them forgiveness, healing acceptance.

The fact that Jesus used the contemporary Jewish picture of what we now call 'hell' to make quite a different point in one of his stories (Dives and Lazarus) should not be taken as a literal description of the eternal alternative to Paradise. The point of the Dives and Lazarus story is that the suffering Dives experiences is of loss, separation and regret. Jesus is urging his hearers to trust and claim God's promises now so as to enjoy fellowship and happiness with God instead of isolation and misery.

Our fears are unfounded. God does love us, will not reject us, will not disappoint us. We may be bad parents and bad children but he is the Good Father who loves his children for what they are: reflections of him through being created in His image.

Fearful thoughts of death can become positive experiences if we allow him to use them to point up where we are going wrong, to re-direct our lives, and to trust and claim his promises.

So we do not enter death alone, we do not enter death for punishment in an alien place, rather we shall experience it as a going home.

Yet even so, there is a sense still of loss or separation, of emptiness and aching yearning. We can be assured that the real sense of loss we experience at death (our own or that of someone close to us) is only temporary. It will not be long before we are again united with those whom we love. Death is only partial. We lose only those parts of us which are failing anyway. The essential 'us' goes on. Death is therefore not so much a loss as a leaving behind of what does not really matter.

The aching yearning we feel is indeed real. But it is not a yearning for what we leave, but for what we are entering. We can easily imagine a similar yearning at the point of birth. Doubtless we thought then it was a yearning to be back in our mother's womb, but was it not really a stronger desire to move into the next phase of our being?

Separation is temporary and partial and we shall afterwards be able to see it as illusory because God has assured us that nothing can separate us from his loving will for us, from his continuing presence.

But this gloomy obsession with death and the association of God with death is darkening our perception of the truth – which is that ours is a God of life, not death, of new beginnings, of happy continuings. The will of the God of life for us is life – life in all its fullness, not death in all its emptiness. Death is his way of drawing us closer to him, not setting us apart, and drawing us closer not on our own but in community with all who share our trust in him.

Nor is it true that we go into death naked and powerless. We take with us those spiritual powers we developed in this part of our existence – the power to discern him, to will him, to enjoy him, to trust him. These powers together represent our faith and it is through that faith that we shall be enabled to recognize the fullness of the life he is holding out to us. It will be through the spiritual powers we are developing in our earth-bound life that we shall be strong enough to swim – or weak enough to float – on the tide of his love to the shores of his kingdom.

So what began as a fearful peep at the next life ends, as do so many of our experiences of God, by bringing us back to the present and to how we live now. We realize that in God we have nothing to be scared of. Death holds no terrors. It is this life and our use of God's gifts to us of this life which is frightening us, or which should be frightening us.

Yet still we want to veer away from painful self-analysis to consider the plight of others. What of those who have not known God or whose experiences of Christianity have been such as to put them off God? We know that not everyone who calls God *Abba* will be recognized as a true son or daughter of God.

Conversely we know that there are God's children in other 'folds' (faiths?) than our own. God would not go to all the loving trouble of bringing people into the world only to destroy or ignore them. They are his children whether or not they know it. For those whose experience of this life, for reasons beyond their control, has not been positive, God, we know, is healing and merciful. The fact that we have experienced rejection – or acceptance – in our own society is therefore no indicator of what we shall receive directly from his hand.

There are a few final things we can confidently say about the next part of life. It will be clearer. The presence and nature and will of God will be undeniable, like the sight of the sun on a clear winter day. By that light, the partiality of our generation's perception of God will be corrected. For example, each generation emphasizes a different aspect of God. Our own generation has stressed familiarity and friendship. We shall have to learn awe and to experience and appreciate that friendship is not just 'jolliness' but is costly and sacrificial.

Again these are things we can begin to learn now. If the gift of God to us in death is to draw us closer to him, our fears of death can also become a gift if we use them to re-direct our attention to the need for change in our lives now. The change that is shown up by our fears of punishment and of separation is that we should turn from self-centredness to God-centredness; from fear of a god we have created in the image of our own bad parenthood to love of the God who is our Good Parent.

We are taken back to first principles, the principles of Christ's commandments that we should love God and love our neighbours as ourselves. These principles take us back from fear and death to hope and life. They take us from our own uncertainties to Christ's clear promise that those who believe in him will not come to judgment but already enjoy eternal life.

Why we are trying to learn to love ourselves

In Part One, we looked at God. We had to be able to believe that he was a God who deserved to be called loving before we could trust ourselves to love him. We had to know that his attitude to us was one of love before we could respond in love.

In Part Two, we have been looking at ourselves. We have seen that we need to be able to value, forgive and love ourselves before we can begin to offer others the appreciation, acceptance and love they too need.

All this has taken us deeper into the first principles outlined by Jesus: to love God and others as we love ourselves.

It has been difficult and painful. We have had to look at our personal responses to the issues raised by AIDS. But it was also necessary and it will prove valuable because it has helped to build up our self-awareness. The more aware we become of ourselves, the more open, sensitive and aware we shall become of others.

The benefits of this experience will begin to show through in all areas of our life, but especially as we seek to help people affected by AIDS.

Of course it is important that we should know, and keep abreast of, the facts about AIDS, but people with AIDS will often know far more about AIDS than their GPs and they do not turn to us in the hope of finding walking encyclopaedias. AIDS is not the centre of our concern – they are.

Of course people with AIDS will need nursing skills and medical treatment, but they do not look to us for these. Their body is not our concern – they are.

Of course we shall be helping them out in little ways like helping with their washing, shopping and cleaning (if that is what they ask us to do) but it is all too easy to make these actions the centre of our ministry when really they should be peripheral to it. People with AIDS do not want our busyness but our stillness, for it is in stillness that we show how comfortable we are with ourselves and with other people.

In this, as in so many other ways, serving the person with AIDS is like every other aspect of our Christian living. We are called to be Christians, not to do Christian things.

Christ's parting words to us were not that he would do things for us but that he would be with us: 'Lo, I am with you always, to the close of the age' (Matt. 28.20). In the same way, when we ask someone with AIDS what we can do to help, he or she often replies, 'Just be with me.' Pascal said something to that effect that the purpose of spirituality is to enable you to be still and at peace with yourself in your own room.

But often we want to replace 'being' with 'doing' so as to keep ourselves busy, because in the stillness of being, we are faced with fears we don't want to face and above all we are faced with our helplessness. The passages you have read and the exercises which follow may help you work through some of these fears by facing them. Then we shall realize that our helplessness, our vulnerability and our own need for acceptance, forgiveness and healing are both useful and appropriate. They are, in fact, the only essential skills we need to be of service to people with AIDS.

Material for prayer and reflection

Whilst this material is intended for group use, some individuals may find it helpful if they are working through the book on their own.

Loving our fears of not being loved or lovable
How do we know we are loved?
What have we experienced of love?
Can we really love others without (or before) loving ourselves?
What is proper self-love?

Loving our sexuality
Why has Western Christianity so often seemed afraid of human sexuality, seeing our sexual needs as part of our 'lower nature'?
How far do you feel you can go along with the author's 'positive Christian sexual ethic'?
What do you wish the church had told you about sexuality at the time you were an adolescent?
If sex is one of God's gifts to us, is this also true for the homosexual's experience of sex?
Is sex, in the final reckoning, a blessing or a curse?

Loving our mortality
When I meet someone with AIDS, do I feel I am meeting someone living with AIDS or dying from AIDS?
If I had AIDS, how might this affect my job, my home, my family, my neighbours, my self-worth?

How do I feel about my own death?
Is it the manner of my dying which frightens me? This could include a fear of the pain or the suddenness or the lack of control I would have over my dying.
Is it the thought of what I will leave behind which frightens me? Perhaps I am really afraid of the effect of my death on those who love and depend on me, or concerned about projects and aims which remain unattempted or incomplete.

Is it what lies beyond death which frightens me? Am I afraid that there may be nothing at all beyond death? Or am I expecting some sort of divine punishment?

The thought of death makes us all aware of our unfinished business. What is yours?
   Who would I want to see again whom I have not seen for years?
   With whom do I need to put things right?
   When have I really told those whom I love how much they mean to me?
   Who would I want with me at the very end?
   Who would I want at my funeral?
   What sort of funeral would I like for myself?
   Write your own funeral oration in two short parts:
(a) your life as you want others to understand it and yourself as you want others to perceive you
(b) what you feel your life has taught you that you want to share with those who survive you.

Recommended reading

   AIDS: Meeting the Community Challenge ed. Vicky Cosstick, St Paul Publications 1987.

Prayer

   This is the prayer of Catholic AIDS Link, a Catholic group offering non-judgmental spiritual, emotional and practical support to those affected by AIDS/HIV.
   Please remember people with HIV related conditions here and throughout the world; their families and friends; those who care for them, the many agencies who offer support and those involved in research.

Blessed are you, our God, for in Jesus you show us the image of your glory. We give thanks for the gospel of healing and liberation which is preached to the whole church in the ministry of those with HIV or AIDS. May we recognize that it is the real body of Christ which suffers at this time through HIV or AIDS. It is the real mind of Christ which is racked by fear and confusion. It is the real image of God in Christ which is blasphemed in prejudice, oppression and poverty.

May we see in this crisis, loving God, not punishment but the place where God is most powerfully at work in Jesus Christ, and where, as sisters and brothers, we can lead each other to life in all its fullness, given in the same Christ our Lord. Amen.

Catholic AIDS Link, PO Box 646, London E9 6QP

Loving Others

Loving Others

Introduction

As Christians, we need to respond to situations both as a community and as individuals. Part Three, therefore, sets out to consider what the response of the Christian community to AIDS could be and how Christians individually could seek to put their faith into action in the service of people affected by AIDS.

Finally, we consider what will be distinctive about the Christian response to AIDS. For those who decide they cannot become more personally involved, there is still work to be done: we all need to be part of a caring and accepting community in which people with AIDS and HIV infection can be supported and valued.

Now that we know that we have only ourselves to give and our faith to rely on, we are ready to offer ourselves in service to people with AIDS. But it is often at this very point that our courage fails us because up to now our decision has been a private one. Now it has to become public. It has been personal. Now it must be shared. We start to prevaricate, to become busy, to put off that commitment until we can find a fence to sit on. But in Christ's kingdom there are no fences to sit on, no sidelines to shout from, only the field and our place in it. We are called to be players, not spectators, referees or commentators. We cannot say to the world's troubles 'These do not affect me. I can't afford to get my hands dirty. I'm not sure. I'd rather not know about it.' If we are Christians, we shall be found not on the touchline, but in the thick of the scrum.

Nor can we face the world's troubles alone and say 'I'll do it my way or not at all.' In this show there are no star turns, we are all part of the chorus. We shall not be thought 'cute' if we stand out and draw attention to ourselves by being out of step. Our concern is not to be noticed but to be effective; not to be glamorous but useful.

Nor will there be any rest until it is over. We cannot walk away to have a little lie-down in the unspoken hope that when we wake up it will have gone away or that our part in it may have been taken over by someone else.

So no excuses. No sick-notes. We are as fit as we have allowed God to make us. We are as ready now as we shall ever be. Our Lord needs us now.

I am firmly convinced that if there is to be a living Christian church in the twenty-first century, it will be because of the work and witness of the church today on the side and in the service of those with AIDS. But if we are found absent or against those with AIDS now, those without AIDS in the future will not even remember whose we claimed to be.

Coming together

We saw in the first part of this book how the partiality of our vision of the world has distorted our vision of God at work in it. Because we have lost sight of our common humanity, we think only of how AIDS is affecting our own society and we forget that it is a global problem. Because we have lost sight of the fact that we are all God's children, we think AIDS is affecting only one part of our family: we tend to think AIDS affects only gay men in Britain. We forget that AIDS affects men, women and children – all our brothers, sisters and their children – around the world. Restoring fullness of vision in this one area has helped us to see how inaccurate and stupid it was to see AIDS as a gay disease and to see AIDS as affecting others and not ourselves.

One of the good things that can come out of AIDS is that it can help us to become aware of these imbalances in our perceptions and can give us a fuller and fairer view of God's world and of his will for that world.

There is, at this point, another imbalance we need to redress. Christianity in the West has increasingly become concerned only with the salvation of individuals. It has therefore lost touch with its Jewish and early-Christian heritage. We have conceived our salvation in purely personal terms: 'I have been concerned with how my soul was saved; how my faith was translated into my actions; how I got to heaven.'

But Abraham was called to start a community; Jesus called his disciples to live in a community with him and with each other. The Acts of the Apostles is very much the story of how individual calls to salvation and discipleship were worked through in the community of believers, the church. St Paul reminds us that we are called as individuals to live together:

> Now there are varieties of gifts, but the same Spirit; and there are varieties of service, but the same Lord; and there are varieties of working, but it is the same God who inspires them all in every one.
>
> For just as the body is one and has many members, and all the members of the body, though many, are one body, so it is with Christ. For by one Spirit we were all baptized into one body – Jews or Greeks, slaves or free – and all were made to drink of one Spirit (I Cor. 12.5,6,12,13).

The call to serve Christ in people with AIDS is a call to each of us as individuals and to us corporately as the community of believers. We are jointly and severally called to repentance, to service and to witness.

We are jointly and severally called to repent of our idolatry. Our society worships the gods of technology, medicine, commerce. Jointly, we rely on our strength and our own power and this gives us a sense of superiority over nature and even over some of our fellow human beings. Severally, we see ourselves as superior to one another: white over black, man over woman, straight over gay, adult over child, able-bodied over handicapped, rich over poor.

We are therefore, as members of our community, sharers in the guilt of our community. Jointly, we have helped to build up and perpetuate social, sexual and racial prejudice and injustice. Jointly, we need to acknowledge this and redirect ourselves. Severally, we have benefited from the oppression and inequalities resulting from these attitudes. Severally, we are better fed, clothed, housed, educated and looked after than those we have downgraded or cast out.

Both as a society and as individuals within that society, we are now suffering the effects of our selfishness and our prejudices. Because we have chosen not to acknowledge all people as our brothers and sisters, we have not shared with our brothers and our sisters in Africa and Asia the advances in medicine we have been enabled to make in Europe and America because of our monopoly of those skills and resources. Consequently, they have been unable to prevent the spread of AIDS. Because we have not shared equally with them the cheap food we enjoy (because we pay them so little to produce it for us), their bodies have been weakened and rendered more prone to disease.

AIDS would not have spread so fast or so far through Africa and would not have reached America or Europe if the societies of America and Europe had shared these God-given resources with the societies of Africa and Asia, and if individuals from Europe and America had not taken sexual advantage of the resultant poverty of individuals from Africa and Asia.

If we ask why some gay people have been particularly prone to this disease, again the answer has to do with injustice and inequality. Some gay people, after years of conditioning, have accepted society's estimation of them as outcast and sub-human and have been driven into furtive, compulsive and degrading means of grasping transitory sexual relief from strangers. It has been our failure as a society to accept and value their difference that has ostracized them. But it is significant that those gay people who have claimed their dignity and independence from our misjudgment of them, and who have sought to enjoy lasting relationships openly, are no more at risk of AIDS than any other faithful couple.

Nor is that all. Having AIDS would not have come to be seen as a socially-ostracizing condition had we not judged others on the basis of too little knowledge and too much prejudice. In other words, it has been our failure as a family to live in generous mutual acceptance and positive loving concern that has turned AIDS into a curse on the whole world family.

This is our shared guilt. We need to acknowledge it, to repent it, and then to begin to put it right. We need to learn to withhold judgment in the future; to condemn the judgmental remarks of our family and friends as soon as we hear them uttered, no matter how socially embarrassing to us this may be.

Then, as a community of Christians, we need to push our churches – locally and nationally – to come out in unequivocal support of people affected by AIDS; to prevent them using AIDS as a stick for queer-bashing or as a goad for chastity; to force them to commit their vast resources of money, buildings, experience, skills, contacts (and above all of people) into the care of those with AIDS and the discovery of a cure for AIDS.

Christians who support national charities need to put pressure on these charities to accept and support this work for and among people with particular opportunistic infections, like Alzheimer's Disease, who just happen to have contracted it as a result of AIDS.

Christians need to make their local church committees or PCCS face these issues and see that for Christ the church exists to welcome and not to ostracize society's outcasts and to make our local Church buildings places where people affected by AIDS will be accepted and our local Christian community a truly caring family into which people with AIDS will be accepted and in which they will be supported.

We need to look at what we mean by community and by family. Before the problem of AIDS, it could be argued that there was no such thing as a gay community. Even now, a lot of gay people do not want to know about the problems of other gay people. It is not just that they don't see themselves as having any connection with these people beyond a common sexuality, they are, by their ostrich-mentality, denying their own gayness. But those who have become involved and concerned are discovering they have more than sexuality in common; that mutual comfort, protection and service unite them and so a real gay community is now discernible.

The church can learn from this. It can learn that community begins with an acknowledgement of our shared humanity and of our need for each other. It can learn that community is built on coming together to share suffering, to offer each other acceptance and value, and of staying together in the service of anyone who hurts. It can learn from the diversity of our sexuality and of the ways in which we express our sexuality, a reflection of the infinitely diverse nature of God's creation and of God's gifts to us. God is not wasteful. He would not have given us so many different gifts if he had not perceived our need of them. It is our task, realizable only in community, to discover why we need so many different gifts and how best to develop and use them.

Up to now, we have not been a family to all God's children: we have sieved and sifted, excluded and rejected. But when two or three people meet regularly in prayer and support of each other in their work for people with AIDS, a new and properly Christian family is born; worship, work and witness go hand in hand; and all are revitalized.

We also need, as voters, to persuade our elected representatives locally, nationally and in Europe, to commit resources on our behalf. We need to find and support those who, nationally and internationally, are putting forward and giving effect to these ideas.

But even in our 'joint doing' what matters most is our 'joint being'. The person with AIDS does need all these things: he needs help with research into the disease; help with treatment, with housing, with employment and so on; he does need his network of friends, but he equally needs a caring community in which he can feel safe and accepted.

Our work in witnessing to the existence and needs of people with AIDS has finally as its aim the changing of attitudes from isolation to community, from segregation to caring acceptance. We are all called to be caring members of a caring community.

What can Christians do together?

Another of the good things to come out of AIDS is that Christians are beginning to learn to pool their skills, experience and resources ecumenically in the face of AIDS. We still have a long way to go before an unwanted building which used to be a Catholic seminary or an Anglican vicarage or a Methodist chapel is given over to the local Aidsline – *without strings attached* – for use as a drop-in centre for prostitutes or a needle-exchange for injecting drug addicts or a place of temporary respite for exhausted carers. But at least, on an individual basis, Christians of different denominations are learning to keep their denominational differences firmly in the background and their service to Christ in their neighbours firmly in the foreground.

The greatest good that could come out of this working together will be when Christians, by being alongside the gay community and learning from their caring example, can also learn to overcome their stereotyped prejudices against all gay people. Then dialogue can begin, the theological issues dividing us can be re-examined, and we can start worshipping together openly as well as working together openly.

We hear a lot in the religious press about a new desire for reconciled unity between different Christian confessions. Let us hope the day soon comes when we hear of an equally urgent yearning from these newly-reunited Christians to embrace all the outcast groups – the very people Christ came to save and chose to serve.

When it comes to finding specific tasks for Christians to do collectively, a word of warning needs to be sounded. Whatever we offer to do needs to start with our coming alongside people with AIDS and listening to them. It is what they want that we should seek to supply, not what we think they ought to want. Many well-intentioned Christian projects for people with AIDS have petered out precisely because they were for (ie on behalf of) and not with the people who were thought to need them.

The other reason for their failing was that they were conceived and executed separately from other AIDS provision locally. No attempt was made to link the work Christians were offering to do into the work already being done by statutory and voluntary bodies. It is essential therefore, when a local Christian community perceives – in consultation with people with AIDS – a gap in existing provision, that it liaise with other local interested bodies and that any action be carried out in the closest co-operation.

Up to now, the provision of care and support services has been necessarily *ad hoc*. There is an urgent need now for co-ordination of effort locally and nationally to see that all need is met and that changing patterns of need are quickly recognized and answered. Parishes can knit themselves into this developing network and co-operate by referring people with AIDS on to local AIDS Helplines. AIDS Helplines need to be able to refer people with AIDS on to parishes for care in the community.

The first thing we can do is to preach and to practise a caring community in which we are all accepted, valued and supported, regardless of our HIV status.

Next, we can recover our ancient and pre-eminent duty of hospitality. We need to remember that the words hotel, hospital and hospice all have a common root which binds Abraham's 'entertainment of angels unawares' (Gen. 18), Christ's teaching on

The Good Samaritan, and the biblical injunctions to care for the stranger. The hospice movement has awakened in some Christians an awareness of its origins not in the care of the dying, but in the provision of houses of rest for pilgrims, travellers, strangers and the destitute.

Since we are all pilgrims on the journey to find meaning in AIDS, to search out the face of Christ in the wasted faces of those living and dying with AIDS, we need to acknowledge that there are other travellers down this road and to recognize that we share with them, if not the same understanding of our journey, at least the same road of service.

Empty vicarages and manses can be renovated and pleasantly furnished and equipped to serve as rest houses to those exhausted by their personal journey. Retreat houses, convents and monasteries need to make contact with local AIDS Helplines and to extend a personal and warm invitation to come for refreshment – without charge. (A lot of volunteers are unemployed. Many people have given up their jobs to care for their sick friends. They cannot afford even the modest prices most religious houses charge visitors, particularly because these houses tend to be situated so far from public transport that only those with cars can reach them.)

The emphasis, though, should be on temporary shelter, on respite care, on providing a short break not a permanent home. Nor will the benefits be only one-way, for the stories of these pilgrims will feed the prayers and inform the thoughts of their hosts.

Such facilities would provide much-needed relief on a planned basis – something for the weary to look forward to. But there is also a need for emergency provision and this is where we can respond as Christian individuals. We have to open not only our hearts but also our homes.

There will be parents who have just found out that their son or daughter is in hospital and who have to travel long distances to visit them. These will be difficult reunions, for the parents may have suffered the double shock of learning not only that their child is facing a life-threatening disease, but is also gay or a drug addict. They will need comfort, informed acceptance, respect, the chance to talk and the chance to keep silent. Above all they will need a warm bed, no fuss, meals at awkward hours and a lift to the local hospital.

There will be parents and lovers and friends who cannot stand the loneliness of going back to an empty house from which their dearest friend has just left for hospital, perhaps never to return. There will be these same loving people, facing the death of their loved one in a state of exhaustion. There will be volunteers who have taken on too much, or who now face strain in their relationships at home through their involvement with people the rest of their families can't stand.

Most of all perhaps there will be Aidsworkers. They take on the huge task of co-ordinating all our efforts; of trying to keep us together when often all we seem able to do is to squabble between ourselves; of enabling us to enable others; of ploughing through mountains of paperwork with the phone constantly ringing and volunteers interrupting and demanding to be noticed; of taking the most appalling slanders and insults from people who are really saying 'I'm frightened. AIDS is coming too close to me. Take it away.' They work for a pittance. They cannot afford the long holidays away they desperately need.

If you have the luxury of a holiday home, offer it to them free of charge and make sure a surprise hamper of food and a few luxuries await their arrival. If you invite them round for a meal, don't drag the conversation back to AIDS or the latest in-fighting. Show them they can trust your confidentiality by never breathing a word of what, in an unguarded moment, they may give vent to. Look out for signs that they are overworked and how you might help ease their burden, but above all, commit yourself to supporting them for they are, often single-handedly, holding the whole show together.

Prayer

Not only shall we want to support people with AIDS and our fellow volunteers with our actions, we shall above all want to support them in prayer. It is for this reason that the whole of Part Five of this book is given over to the subject of prayer. This section, however, is not concerned with the substance but the organization of that prayer.

When you get involved in any activity related to AIDS you will become part of a system carefully designed to support you in off-loading problems, being affirmed and accepting constructive criticism. You need to ensure a parallel system of prayerful Christian support.

There are two ways you might like to consider. The first is by setting up or joining a prayer cell and the second is by joining an organization specifically set up to approach AIDS from a spiritual dimension.

The prayer cell. The word 'cell' reveals both the danger and the potential of this approach. A prayer cell becomes a prison cell if it becomes exclusive and cuts you off from others. You need to discover all the Christians working in your local Aidsline or AIDS Helpline and invite them to join with you in regular prayer for everyone affected by AIDS, including our own work as volunteer helpers. The group should not exclude people of other denominations but should aim to encourage as wide a Christian membership as possible. But to be effective it does need to remain local.

It is the concerns of the local Aidsline and of people with AIDS locally that will be the subject of your prayers. Occasional guest speakers will help broaden your outlook, but most of the time you will be just praying as a small group of local friends. One way to organize a typical session would be for two members to prepare a theme. One of them will lead prayers and the other give a short address on what they feel, from their experience of work with people with AIDS, is paramount to them about this ministry, or perhaps they may prefer to lead a Bible study. (Many of the Bible passages used in this book could be helpful, particularly those in Parts 1, 4 and 5). Each session should contain time for fellowship, prayer, study, sharing and silence. It is in silence that healing begins.

To prevent the group becoming too introspective, and to help group members keep a perspective on their work and worries, it could be helpful for the group to link up to a national organization and to make contact with and actively support an AIDS project in the so-called Third World.

In these ways the dangers of the 'prison cell' may be overcome and the idea broaden out into that of a 'monastic cell', a place of retreat for contemplation and meditation. But the idea can broaden even further.

The other 'cell' we may think of in this context is the cell of a honeycomb. This may lead us to want to link up our work of prayer to that of other local prayer groups. In particular, since our work is part of Christ's healing ministry, we may want to link up with other healing prayer groups and to extend our support of Third World AIDS projects to include work in the Third World for people with leprosy – a salutary reminder to us that forty years after a cure for leprosy was found we are still faced with massive numbers of people infected because so many societies will not face the ugly reality of the disease in their midst.

But our work is also part of Christ's proclaiming ministry, so we may want to link up with local mission committees as well. The possibilities are endless and the variety they introduce will refresh and re-focus our prayers for people with AIDS. Some may wish to open membership of their prayer cell to people of other faiths, giving expression to our common suffering and our common search for healing. But whomever we do or don't invite to join us, there is one problem we must address. That is the problem of confidentiality.

There will be things we need to share, things people have said to us, situations in which we have found ourselves, things we have noticed. Possibly, by accident, names will be dropped. Or, to make it clear what we mean, we may have to describe a situation in such detail that the rest of the group can guess which hospital or organization, which volunteer or doctor we mean.

Before the group really gets underway, therefore, it is essential that every member publicly promises totally to respect outside the group the utter confidentiality of what is said inside the group. This is not to set up a secret organization, but to recognize and respect that such is the state of society at the moment that the slightest hint that a person is antibody-positive is enough to jeopardize their job and home security.

Whether we work in a small cell of local volunteers or in a larger cell of caring people of all faiths, our object is the same: to offer up to God our own suffering, bewilderment, anger and sorrow in order that he can heal us; and to invite his blessing that we may, through him, become instruments of his healing to others; and to pray for the healing of our society and of those within our community who have AIDS.

National organizations. As individuals, or as members of a prayer cell, we need to know that there are other Christians working nationally on our behalf and doubtless we shall want to support them and be supported by them. In the Church of England, the

Church in Wales, and the Church of Scotland, the first point of contact should be with the Diocesan Board of Social Responsibility, where you should find one person with responsibility for AIDS.

Quakers, as always, are quietly working away where the need is greatest and Methodists can at least take pride in having produced the most positive and loving leaflet on AIDS yet to be available from any church. Written by Michael Jebson for the Methodist Association of Youth Clubs and published by The Methodist Church Division of Education and Youth, it helps young people who want to face the challenge of AIDS and 'live without fear'.

Catholic Aids Link is a Catholic group nationwide, offering non-judgmental, spiritual, emotional and practical support to those affected by HIV or AIDS. It also links people up by means of a regular attractive and useful Newsletter. Write to them care of: PO Box 646, London E9 6QP.

CARA (Care & Resources for People Affected by AIDS/HIV) is a London-based pastoral ministry, non-denominational, offering, in addition to pastoral care, educational training and theological and spiritual reflection, working with other agencies in all aspects of its work including the practical use of resources (such as buildings) in caring for people with HIV/AIDS. Write to them at: The Basement, 178 Lancaster Road, London W11 1QU.

Christian Action on Aids has five main aims:

1. To extend awareness, particularly among Christians, of what AIDS is – its nature, its extent and its consequences.

2. To help Christians and others reflect biblically and theologically on the issues raised by AIDS.

3. To create awareness in the churches of what needs to be done both here and overseas: in encouraging and enabling education about AIDS and its implications in promoting the development of counselling for those affected in whatever way; in raising public consciousness of the immense financial costs which are already arising for additional medical care.

4. To support people with AIDS; to help overcome prejudice and ignorance and to extend the love of Christ, in prayer and action, to those in need in this area.

5. To act as a co-ordinating resource agency for the churches and seeking from the churches a considered response and programme for action.

In seeking to realize these aims, the CAA produces 'Rainbow Ribbons' which we are encouraged to wear to demonstrate our love and compassion for the tragic human suffering and loss of lives as a result of this epidemic. Write to: The Administrator, Christian Action on AIDS, PO Box 76, Hereford HR1 1JX.

One of the worst consequences of the association of AIDS with gay people has been the increase in the number of violent and hysterical attacks on gay people. This has also happened within the church and no one has suffered from it more than the *Lesbian and Gay Christian Movement*. The LGCM has four main aims:

1. To encourage fellowship, friendship and support among individual gay Christians through prayer, study and action, wherever possible in local groups and especially to support those gay Christians subjected to discrimination.

2. To help the whole church re-examine its understanding of human sexuality, and to work for a positive acceptance of gay relationships within the framework outlined in their Statement of Conviction, so that all homosexuals may be able to live without fear of rejection or recrimination, and that homosexual Christians may be able to contribute fully to the life and ministry of the church.

3. To encourage members to witness to their Christian faith and experience within the gay community, and to witness to their convictions about human sexuality within the church.

4. To maintain and strengthen links with other gay Christian groups both in Britain and elsewhere.

Christian justice as well as Christian compassion demand better treatment for this courageous and ill-used group. They may be contacted at: LGCM, BM 6914 London WC1N 3XX.

When writing to any of these groups, please enclose a large stamped addressed envelope and state clearly the information you require. Please allow at least a fortnight for reply as most of these groups are run by volunteers.

What can Christians do individually?

The first point to make is that we must not try to do it alone. Tempted as we may be by shyness or ideological conviction not to join in with

83

existing provision, the dangers and problems of going it alone are insuperable.

Firstly, God does not want us to go it alone. He wants us to join with him. He also wants us to join with other Christians. But his definition of one of his followers is probably different from ours. Just as we all know there are Christians who go to church but whose behaviour in no way merits their being described as Christian, so we know there are people who would never dream of describing themselves as Christian but who seem, by everything they say and (more importantly) do, to be so much closer to Christ than we are. God's friends may not be our friends. They may not be the friends of our version of Christianity. But because they are known to him and are already co-operating with him to bring comfort and relief to those suffering, we should join up with them, learn from them and support them.

Secondly, if we do not join up with our local AIDS support services (variously called Aidslines/AIDS Helplines, etc), we shall not be able to get into contact with people with AIDS. Nor shall we know what services are available to help them. We could easily end up duplicating existing services or depriving people of better help from other sources than we can offer.

At this point you may well not feel adequate to the task ahead, nor even be clear what that task will be for you. Take heart. Humility and self-awareness are the only essential prerequisites for this work because they force us to acknowledge our need of training to turn concern into action and support to maintain our commitment.

Training

Effective training can only be given by people who have had personal experience of the issues, who continue to be involved alongside the people affected by these issues and who have skills in training others. It has to be said that such people are few and far between. Charlatans abound. But the safest way of getting good, practical training is to contact your nearest AIDS Helpline. Because the addresses and phone numbers of these organizations change so often, it is not possible to include a full list here. Instead, phone the National AIDS Helpline on 0800 567123, which is a 24-hour service. Explain that you want to join a local AIDS organization as a volunteer and ask them how you can get in touch with your nearest one.

Phone your local number, say you want to apply for training to be a volunteer and ask them to send you an application form. Each Aidsline will operate a different way. Some will send you a form. Others will invite you in for a chat. All will want to know why you want to help and how you think you can be of use.

Be prepared for some delay between your applying and your being offered training or even an interview. All the Aidslines I know are short-staffed and working under tremendous pressure. Training is carried out mainly by experienced volunteers and the time they take out to train you is time they take away from people with AIDS. Training is therefore precious. If you are offered a place on a course, cancel everything else in order to attend.

Training will be hard. It will help prepare you to face the questions of the 'worried well' and to share the terror of those who have just discovered they are antibody positive. It will enable you to share the pain of those who have AIDS and to support their lovers, families and friends, among whom will be your fellow volunteers. The aim of the training will be to develop a team of volunteers with a common philosophy capable of being flexible and responsive to the changing needs of people affected by AIDS. At the end of the training, if you are invited to join the volunteers running an Aidsline, you will be offered a variety of ways in which to come alongside people with AIDS. Again, these will vary according to the different groups, but they may include:

Telephone counselling

The principal contact point between the service and the public is a telephone number which is staffed at certain times of the day or evening. This enables members of the public to get information and advice without compromising their anonymity. Your job would be to provide callers with the means to make decisions for themselves. It is much more directive than Samaritan counselling. You are there to give advice and information as much as to give support. You will therefore need to keep abreast of all news and developments as well as of all rumours and myths. You will need to be able to make a minimum commitment (say one evening a month) to staffing the phonelines and more time to ongoing training.

Befriending

There are now several models for providing a system of individual support for people with AIDS. The best of these models allows the person with AIDS to choose who shall be their 'buddy' and insists that the buddy is him/herself part of a network of carers, supported by a network of carers. Your commitment then is to befriend that person for the rest of their life as and when they ask you. It is not your job to swamp them with your affection, nor to wear yourself out fetching and carrying for them, but to be with them all the way. Make sure before you begin that the befriending system has been set up in the way that local people with AIDS perceive their needs and also make sure you have your own back-up support system of people who are there for you while you are being there for your friend. The commitment in befriending someone is total. Without adequate supervision and support you should not begin to attempt it. You would anyway be well advised not to begin this type of work in your first two years as a volunteer.

Family support

Those who care deeply for someone with AIDS or HIV also need support. In some ways, their need for support is even greater than that of the person who is HIV+ or who has AIDS, for at least these people will be offered counselling on their visits to hospitals for check-ups or treatment and they will almost certainly be put in touch with local AIDS services. There is even a danger here in that they can begin to feel that what makes them important is that they have AIDS. Caring people will fall over backwards to smother them with affection and, perhaps because elsewhere they would be rejected, they may enjoy staying in the warmth of this uncritical attention. But AIDS gives no one the right to be hurtful to others, rude or selfish. It is the person not the disease that is special and Christians will have to bear this in mind as they seek to help people affected by AIDS come to a properly balanced self-perception.

Because of this concentration on people affected by AIDS, we sometimes forget that for every person with AIDS there must be at least ten people indirectly affected. These may include that person's lover or partner, their friends and their family. Family Support Groups are for all these people. They provide what is often the only opportunity these people may have to come together and support each other, whether their relationship to the person they love is that of husband, wife, lover, friend, mother, father, sister or brother. It is the amount you love that person that matters and not the name society gives to your relationship.

From the volunteer's point of view, this is very demanding work and few will find it very rewarding. The families come together for regular meetings, but the volunteer's job in these meetings is merely to facilitate the group – to make sure a place is provided where they will feel warm and safe; to make hot drinks and provide a warm welcome; to listen; to share; and then to let go.

This is particularly hard when you know that people are often going back to difficult, lonely and painful situations. Volunteers may give the families their home phone numbers but should not initiate any contact outside the group meeting, for this would be to intrude on the families' privacy. If they want help, they will phone you. If they do not phone you, you have to hope that no news is good news or come to terms with the fact that yours was not the help they needed or wanted.

The work of the volunteer in supporting families is very much that of making oneself available, and since this inevitably means making oneself vulnerable, it can hurt.

I have described this work in slightly more detail than other sections simply because this is the newest and fastest-growing of all support services and this fact alone should show us how desperately needed such support is. The worst Family Support Groups are those in which the volunteers do the supporting. The best are those in which the families are enabled to support each other.

Raising awareness

Many Aidslines offer education and training services to the local voluntary sector. These aim to raise awareness of the facts of AIDS and the needs and rights of people affected by AIDS and so to help build a caring and accepting community. Volunteers with training and communication skills are much needed to train those who have influence over housing policy, the provision of social services, over children and young people in educational and residential settings, over the type and quality of care for people with AIDS in hospitals and in the community, over the press and over the churches.

Self-help

Perhaps the most important work for people with AIDS is done by other people with AIDS. In different areas groups will have different names but you may hear of *Frontliners*, people with AIDS who support and encourage each other; *Body Positive*, again a national organization with many regional branches where people who are antibody-positive support each other.

Some of these groups have support groups of people who do not have AIDS or do not think they are antibody positive and these people raise money for the group, publicize its existence and services, and provide whatever help people in the group feel they need. They may also have a painful but necessary role to play in bearing the brunt of group members' distrust of carers generally while at the same time trying to help members to keep a proper balance about confidentiality. After all, support is a mutual thing and trust is the risk we have to take to stay in touch with each other.

Special issues

One of the ways Aidslines stay flexible to the changing needs of the general local population and of those affected by AIDS locally is by setting up *ad hoc* groups to deal with specific issues. For instance, in one area, the care of prisoners who are antibody positive may be vital, both while they are in a prison and even more so upon their release. Making contact with prostitutes (who, incidentally, appear to be more at risk of catching AIDS from their boyfriends than from their clients) may be a major local concern. Or groups may be set up to monitor and advise on AIDS issues affecting particular groups – women, teenagers, injecting drug users, etc.

Fund-raising

No one seems to join an Aidsline in order to raise money but there would be no Aidslines to join unless money was raised. Aidslines receive some funding from statutory sources but all depend on their own efforts to improve and extend the services they offer. It is incumbent upon every volunteer to help to raise the money needed both by urging statutory agencies to give more realistically and by urging local people to give towards a service which is provided free of charge to them and for them. However, it does have to be said that an inordinate love of the power that money brings is often at the root of many of the problems within voluntary organizations of all sorts. I have yet to be convinced that more money brings better services to those on whose behalf the money was raised.

Time and talents

You should now look at your time and your talents and decide how you will use them in the service of people affected by AIDS. Are you going to join local caring people – Christian and non-Christian – and work co-operatively in the community or exclusively within the church? Are you going to do telephone or face-to-face counselling? Hospital visiting or community caring? Are you going to spend most of your time educating the public in the matters raised by AIDS, or in 'buddying'?

Perhaps the best decision is to try out several areas and progress from one to another as you become more involved and more experienced. Constantly ask yourself whether what you are doing is actually what people with AIDS have asked of you and not what you think they ought to want.

For the Christian, though, it is not just a matter of deciding where our talents and limitations lie. Nor is it simply a matter of working out how much time we can commit to this cause. We have to face the fact that most of the organizations already set up to help people affected by AIDS have not been set up as overtly Christian. Indeed, many of them would argue that if they had put 'Christian' anywhere in their title, this would have put off the people most in need.

In your training, you will, if you have been open about your faith, probably already have faced some suspicion if not hostility. It is part of the guilt we must bear that other Christians have, by their explicit condemnation of homosexuality or by their implicit rejection of homosexuals, left such people with nowhere to turn for comfort. It could well be argued that society has followed the lead of the church in condemning homosexual life-styles and thereby forced homosexuals into furtive and dangerous ways of seeking sexual contact which have placed them at risk of acquiring many diseases, including AIDS.

Christians have forfeited the right to lead the way in the care of homosexuals with AIDS, and because Christians have followed others in assuming that people with AIDS are either promiscuous or homosexual or both, Christians have further forfeited the right to lead the way in caring for other people with AIDS.

The AIDS organizations have been set up precisely because the church was providing nothing. It ill behoves us now to attempt to take over these organizations and still less to set up our own parallel organizations, unless these are set up at the express wish of people affected by AIDS and work co-operatively with any existing voluntary provision.

What will be distinctive about our Christian service?

Now that we have thought through the issues and committed ourselves to positive action; sought and obtained the training we need and decided to express our concern in co-operation with existing work, we are ready to begin.

We have sought the support of God and of each other not for a particular caring action, but for a particular way of caring. We therefore now need to ask ourselves what will be distinctive about our ministry.

To start you on the road to finding your own answer to that question, the rest of this chapter is in the form of three reflections on how a Christian might re-act in three situations in which AIDS volunteers often find themselves:
 – faced with someone who is homeless
 – faced with someone suicidal
 – faced with visiting someone in hospital.

They are not offered as a pattern for Christian ministry but as a mirror to help you answer how you are going to seek and respond to Christ in your friend and how he is going to seek and respond to Christ in you.

Homelessness

AIDS raises many issues – of justice, poverty, illness and sin and the relationship between them, sex and death and the relationship between them – but perhaps most clearly it shows up our attitudes to people who don't fit society's expectations of what is acceptable and respectable.

Coming alongside people with AIDS has proved, for me, an

opening-up exercise. Visiting people in hospital with AIDS-related illnesses has helped me visit people at home or in hospital with other diseases; it has helped me recognize the dis-ease in people who think themselves healthy; and it has helped me cope better with my own dying and death and so with my own living and life. In no area is this clearer than in relation to home and homelessness.

People with AIDS and people who are HIV+ may well experience homelessness for some or all of the time. They may have been homeless before they discovered they were HIV+. Or they may share the news of their HIV status with the family or friends they are living with and find themselves thrown out. Or someone may reveal their HIV status to their landlord. Or their landlord may guess. Or they may lose their job through illness or discovery and not be able to keep up the mortgage repayments. Whatever the cause, the result is the same.

But people with HIV/AIDS are not the only ones made homeless. All homeless people are more at risk of AIDS. Without a home you don't have the same facilities to maintain your own or your family's hygiene. The pressures of being homeless or of being forced to share squalid housing with many others may lead you to seek escape in drugs. The desperate need for more money to change your situation may lead you to prostitution. We can't condemn them. We can't say 'I wouldn't'. We don't know. We are not, thank God, in their situation.

My problem is not that I don't know what it is like but that I don't want to know. I have been homeless. I have known what it feels like to have a creeping numbness overpower the panic as I stood on a pavement with a suitcase and nowhere to go. I have known the rising tide of anger and frustration and despair of tramping from one government department to another and from one charity to another as I tried to find somewhere to live and some way of paying for it.

Admittedly I have not known what it feels like to hear a landlady say 'No blacks' or 'No DHSS', but I have felt my mind retreat from reality into a fantasy world of ideal homes in ideal settings to disguise my sheer powerlessness to change anything in my real situation. Yet still I do not know how it feels to be really homeless.

I was lucky. I was taken in by friends. I know what it feels like to live on charity, but that is different. It is disempowering and belittling but it is not anything like as destructive to one's self-worth as feeling one is so much jetsam, which is what someone literally on the streets must feel.

So my problem is not that I don't know but that I don't want to know. I can look at someone who has AIDS and say 'It's not his fault' – and mean it. But I can't look at someone who is homeless and say 'It's not his fault.' Something inside me shouts 'It must be his fault. Everyone has a home who deserves one.'

If I am asked to give a home – for a night or for life – to someone who is HIV+, I ask: will we get on, will it make him happy, is mine the right home for him? These questions help me practically work out the process of freeing a room in my home and space in my life for that person.

But if I am told they are homeless – whether or not they are HIV+ – I find myself saying 'no' . . . and then searching for justifications. Why did he lose his home? What did he do to get himself thrown out? Why doesn't he have a job? Why come to me?

Because homelessness affects so many people with AIDS/HIV, you will be asked as a volunteer if you could help, possibly by making a room in your house available for overnight or more long-term use. So this question will affect you. Perhaps my experience will help you sort out how you will answer.

I provided a home for a very short time to a young and very attractive male prostitute who was homeless. He was also a thief. He tried repeatedly to seduce a member of my household. He wasn't at all shy at telling my visitors what he did for a living. He had been very severely traumatized as a child and would wake up every hour in the night screaming or moaning loudly. What started out as compassion turned to farce, which quickly turned to tragedy. I couldn't cope and bundled him off somewhere else.

Why couldn't I cope? I think the main reason was that I felt I should be able to cope. I was acting out of duty, not out of love. I wasn't admitting to myself my own prejudices and the limits of my love. I felt I was – or should be – a ministering angel. I wasn't any sort of angel – and anyway, he didn't want an angel.

There was of course more to it than that. I was being nosey. I had a ghoulish fascination with strange life-styles. I wanted to know what made him tick. I had no right to know. He had no need to tell me. I therefore felt hurt and rejected and this led me to look for reasons to reject him.

When he told my friends and neighbours that he was a prostitute, they took a different view of my 'do-gooding' and I could not cope with their misunderstanding my motives (or had they seen me more clearly than I wanted them to, or than I wanted to see myself?) I needed their praise and acceptance, not their gossip and rejection.

And when he stole, screamed, seduced . . . I pretended I didn't know he was testing me; that his experience of being rejected was so complete, nor that his need to put down roots and be accepted was just as great as mine; and that because of this he felt he had to make sure how he stood before he dared to care enough to open up and settle down. So I rejected him and added to his sense of being rejectable. Once he held up an empty Coke can, said 'That's me', then crushed it and tossed it aside.

What would Jesus have done?, I often wonder. The answer is easy. He was careful not to have a home during his ministry, so he didn't need to worry about guests ruining the saucepans and sheets and bothering the neighbours and children.

But actually sharing the homelessness of others made life harder not easier for him, because wherever he went visiting he had to take his disciples and camp-followers with him. I imagine him turning up at Mary and Martha's house in Bethany.

'Hello,' he says, 'could I stay the night? By the way, I've brought my friends with me . . . Well no, actually, they're not very respectable. I've got a couple of fishermen – nice blokes but a bit clumsy, so don't put out the best china. Very loud too – I don't call them "Sons of Thunder" for nothing! No? Well, how about a Zealot? Well yes, they are armed terrorists, but . . . Hang on, I've just remembered. I do have two quiet middle-class blokes. One's from the Inland Revenue – fallen on hard times. No? Well the other one is very well-educated, very respectable, from an excellent family. You will? Thanks. Let me introduce you: Mary and Martha, this is Judas.'

Suicide

You work as a volunteer on a telephone counselling service for people worried about AIDS. It's been a bad day and now the evening seems to stretch endlessly away. Someone you have grown to love has taken a long time to die and too much of you feels to have died with her. For the last few weeks you had been praying 'Put her out of her misery', meaning 'Put me out of the misery I feel at watching her die and not being able to do anything about it.' Euthanasia has come to seem a compellingly humane option. In fact, tonight you feel that anyone learning they have AIDS should be issued with a suicide pill in case they want to use it.

The phone rings and wakes you from your reverie. On the line is a young man. You say your bit. There is a long pause. Then, his voice shaking, he says:

'I've just got the results from my test. I've got AIDS. I want to die.'

And you think: 'Why not?'

As if reading your thoughts, he says: 'Just give me one reason to go on living!'

What can you say? 'Your dying won't solve anything.'

'Says who?'

'It'll hurt those you love and who love you.'

'Will it? Will it hurt them more or less than being told I'm dying of the world's most unspeakable disease?'

Anyway, in this situation it is his hurt and not theirs that counts. Should I say: 'No one has that right.'

Or is that the last resort of the unimaginative – when you can't think of a reason, recite a rule?

So instead I said: 'What's stopping you?'

It's funny that I need to justify that. But I do. I felt he literally meant what he said: please help me work through this feeling until I can find a reason not to die. I might have been right. I was reassured by remembering that suicide is the frequent reaction of people on learning their HIV status.

I tried to picture him out there in the dark, alone in a phone box, with no one else to turn to or talk to. He must have been feeling as lonely and isolated as one imagines one will in death. He was simply associating tonight's loneliness and isolation with the loneliness and isolation of the grave. He wasn't so much saying 'I want to die' as recognizing that he was dying.

He felt powerless. He was going to die because the doctors had said so, or because the newspapers had said so or because the disease said so. His body was in a state of civil war and he had lost the fight, whichever side won.

Helping him to see that regarding himself in negative imagery was only worsening the situation was something he was not yet ready to hear. For now my task was to help him regain a sense of control over his life.

But that meant acknowledging that he did have the power to end his life – he did have the right to make that choice. According to my moral code, he did not have the right to follow that decision through into action. But my moral code was irrelevant. I had to find out his moral code; what had kept him living until now.

I believe that it is not the diagnosis of HIV that creates the idea of suicide in someone's mind. Rather, the diagnosis brings to a head a long process of low self-esteem, of growing despair at the potential of life to be loving and worth living.

So I went back to his original statement and asked him how he knew he had AIDS. He was as puzzled as perhaps you are. But the reason is simple enough.

Anyone being tested for the presence in their blood of the antibodies to the HIV virus which can cause AIDS is counselled before and after they are tested. One purpose of this counselling is to explain that a positive result does not mean they have AIDS. It does not even mean that they will go on to develop AIDS. It means that they have been exposed to the virus but that their immune system is already fighting back by producing antibodies to destroy that virus or at least to render it harmless. No one can tell how successful their immune system will be. No one can predict the outcome. But a positive result, despite all this advice, is still often interpreted by the person who is discovered to be HIV+ as a diagnosis of AIDS.

So the first thing to note about the young man on the phone is that he had *decided* he had AIDS. In a very real sense he had *chosen* to have AIDS. Against all medical knowledge, against all the advice, he had *elected* to die. All those years of rejection and guilt and self-loathing had found in that diagnosis an explanation to justify a long-held death wish.

So it was not the moment of diagnosis but that moment seen as the culmination of his lifetime's experience that had added up to a conscious or unconscious awareness that for him life was not worth living. Perhaps he had sought love and lost it or not found it. Perhaps he had sought acceptance and been rejected. Certainly he had found something in himself which other people did not like (or would not like if he had dared reveal himself) and he had conspired with them to reject him. He found himself an outcast and believed himself to deserve this ostracism. No one liked him. He did not like himself. It was not a case of the chicken and the egg but of experience and self-awareness growing side by side and confirming each other.

Whether he hoped for better things in the next life or wanted to punish himself (or us) for not having made a success out of this life, he saw death as the final and inevitable stage in this process of self-rejection.

But the assumption behind such a suicide is that death will end the feelings of isolation and rejection. The Christian viewpoint is probably that such a death would only confirm these feelings. If he did not love or value himself, he would not allow even God to love him because his self-rejection would lead him eternally to reject all God's loving overtures.

So it is not just the trauma of receiving a positive diagnosis, I suggest, which makes someone feel suicidal. If a person who is otherwise happy with their life discovers they are HIV+, they may well feel suicidal, but more out of shock than self-loathing. Their suicidal threat is real, but with help it would probably pass. Suicide is literally life-threatening for those who have in some sense already given up on life and on themselves, people who feel themselves meriting their experience of rejection.

What I had to do was to help this young man feel himself loved so that he might come to see himself capable of love for himself. But my loving him must involve accepting him unconditionally and that meant that I had, for now, to accept his decision, recognizing that it was a decision made a long time ago.

My one straw of hope was that at last his death wish was being vocalized. It could now be acknowledged and explored. For perhaps the first time, he was admitting how he felt about himself – about what had happened to him more than about what might happen to him – and he wanted to share that with a fellow human being.

Now it is not the purpose of this book to offer the reader a potted course in suicide counselling, even were such a thing possible or desirable. But it is important that we look at suicide and ask how we feel about it, because suicide is an important issue for many people who are HIV+.

However, I have used story rather than theory as the way in to discussing suicide because it is important we don't divorce suicide from the person who is feeling suicidal. We have to feel our way forward, not think our way out of it.

So how, as Christians, do we feel about suicide?

If we were to define sin as anything the effect of which is to distance us to a greater or lesser degree from God, and if we can leave out of 'sin' any other connotation it has acquired for us, then, for me, suicidal would still be sinful.

If I killed myself I would be rejecting a gift from God, the gift of life. I would also be cutting myself off from God and from the possibility of his healing me. I am not saying that God could not find a way round that, and I am sure he would want to try, but my action would make his job that much harder. So for me suicide is personal sin. But it is also communal sin.

We would all share responsibility for the experience of life which built up in that individual a sense that he was not loved. And whose would be the greater sin? His for thinking that when he has AIDS we shall love him less than we love him now? Or ours for helping to build up in him this certainty of rejection?

The man on the phone ran out of coins. I took his number and rang him back. There was no reply.

At the funeral of someone whom the family had probably suspected of being gay (but it was never said, not even to him) and who had died suddenly (it was suicide, but it was never said) and who had been very worried about his own health after his friend (really his lover, but it was never said) died of a disease which was never named, one aunt said to no one in particular – for so presumably she regarded me – 'Perhaps it was for the best.'

Is that how we really feel?

Would we really prefer the difficult and the painful (situations and people) to just go away?

And if we do, do we also imagine they do not feel this?

There are those in my experience whose suicide has been the last pathetic attempt to do what those who 'loved them' wanted.

Hospital visiting

Few people find hospital visiting easy, especially when visiting someone with a very serious illness. The 'story' of how difficult each visit is has been told in the section 'Loving our feelings'. That took us from travelling to the hospital to the anxiety as one waits outside the ward and wishes one could be anywhere else. This section is concerned with the visit itself. It looks at a biblical source of inspiration for hospital (or any sick) visiting and then seeks to translate this into practice.

It has always struck me as marvellous that Job, the book of suffering, should come just before Psalms, the book of praise. This is also true to our experience, for we know that when we let suffering become a source of encounter with God, that encounter heals us and our anger and despair turn gradually to praise and thanksgiving.

As far as the man himself is concerned, what stands out for me about Job was not that he cursed the day of his birth and demanded an explanation from God. It is certainly not the hopeless and unintentionally cruel advice of his friends. What stands out is that rightly or wrongly he sees God as the ultimate source of everything that happens to him.

It is God who gives and God who takes away (Job 1.21). Job's suffering extends his experience of God. Good and evil, he is led to understand, we receive at the hand of God (Job 2.10). Even his demand for an arbitrator to judge between him and God is an acknowledgement that in every aspect of his life, but particularly in his suffering, God and he are bound; that God is not standing apart from his pain; that all the misery and injustice in the world looks to God for relief, reparation and justice because God is just.

The Prologue (Job 1.1–22; 2.1–8) – a secret aside shared with the reader but not with Job – points to Job's election to suffering. This election is not seen as punishment but as a unique honour. Job was a 'blameless' man, 'upright'. Job feared God and had turned from evil (1:1). God loves him so much that he boasts of him to Satan (1.8 and 2.3). God allows Satan to test Job, but only so far. At first Satan is allowed to hurt anything but Job's life (1.12). Later, Satan is allowed to hurt Job's body but must spare his life.

However we understand from this prologue, it is clear that Job is given the honour of showing the integrity of his faith through suffering; that God allows but does not will that suffering; and that God limits that suffering.

Part of Job's suffering – a large part – is to have to listen to the advice of his friends and co-religionists. It is worth pointing out that Job is silent until they sit down beside him! We note in 2.11 that they had come to condole with him and to comfort him. For a whole week they do just that. Verse 13 tells us that when they saw how great was his suffering, they just sat with him day and night for a week . . . but as soon as Job opened his mouth, they just had to butt in. Straightaway all thought of offering him comfort goes out of the window. They attack him for hidden sins, for apostasy, for a lack of faith, for holding the wrong faith, for being human.

There is an important lesson here for those who would care for people with AIDS. What those who are suffering need is not our understanding of the reasons for it all but our understanding of them and what they need: the comfort and condolence that come from our simply being there so completely with the person who is ill that we can bear to be together in silence. Too often it is our words that separate us from those we love and want to support, or it is our words which distance us from the smell of the sick room. Words are used to evade heartfelt but unspoken states of feeling. So if you can't bear to be silent, keep away.

Jesus asks of his disciples different things at different points in his ministry. At the beginning he asks them to 'follow'. Throughout his ministry he asks them to 'do as I do', but at the end, in his deepest need, he asks them simply to be with him: 'stay awake', 'be alert', 'watch and pray'.

Being there to be invited in

We are called to be there for our friend who is ill. What does this mean?

Firstly it means being available for whenever our friend needs us and letting him know that we are available. It means going to see him as often or as rarely as he invites us. It means leaving before he gets tired, unless he has asked us to stay until he is asleep.

Secondly, being there is not a matter of duty or rota but of responding to an invitation. We may 'be there' for someone without ever being invited in. So be it. We are called as servants of God to wait on God. That means that we have to hang around, resisting the temptation to while away the time in 'busyness' lest we miss the call when it does come; to be alert and lively to the possibility of being called. It does not mean that we will be called every time. That is not required of us. But to wait expectantly, that is our Christian calling.

On being invited in

When and if we are invited in, it is to be of service to him. We have first to recognize the one who is calling us. Christ not only bids us enter; he not only asks us to mediate his loving concern through our loving actions so that the 'patient' recognizes him in us, but he also asks us to recognize him in the 'patient'. We wait in Christ on our friend and we wait on Christ in our friend.

This at least will help us avoid the mistake of Job's friends. They assumed he knew nothing of God or God of him. They set out to 'put him straight' from the vast store of their knowledge about God. And they were completely useless precisely because their knowledge was about God (head knowledge, facts picked up along the way and absorbed without being understood) and not of God (heart knowledge, personal experience of a living relationship). Consequently what they said about God was wrong.

We can learn from this to recognize that Christ already knows our friend and only to speak of Christ to our friends when we are bidden – and even then, only to speak in so far as we know him.

It follows that we have to find out how our friend experiences Christ. He may well not call him Christ. This should not trouble us. Christ is in each of us whether or not he is recognized for who he is or called by the name we know him by. The Christ our friend has experienced may be hope, companionship, compassion, or a sense of the numinous. He may be called Allah or Buddha or Marx.

If Job's friends had taken the trouble to ask and listen and learn what Job knew of God, and of the cause and purpose of his suffering, how different an experience for Job that suffering would have been.

So if our friend blames God or demands of God answers to his situation, then it is not for us to answer on God's behalf. All we can do is to help him recognize God in him; put him in touch with that experience and suggest that he ask those questions of God. Perhaps we can add, 'I don't know. All I do know is that God cares for you enough to have sent me to share what you're going through and to have inspired thousands of his followers around the world to be praying for you at this moment.'

Finding the right words

It is really a matter of learning our friend's language and learning to speak in his language. The clipped and cryptic jargon of any religion is ambiguous enough for our co-religionists: it is virtual jibberish to outsiders. To talk of salvation and redemption, or of sin or heaven, is to show our friend that we don't care or know enough about what we are saying to be able to translate it into terms within his experience and that he does not matter enough to us for us to take the trouble to find out if these words are relevant or meaningful to him. We are imposing our world-view on him. We are defending ourselves instead of arming him, just as Job's friends clung to a God of their own making for their own security.

Language is important for it reveals how we feel about what we are saying. Consider whether each time you have come across the phrase 'a person with AIDS' you have unconsciously slurred it into PWA (our slang – it reduces him to a statistic, a type) or 'patient' (already you've put him in hospital and begun to play doctors and nurses, with you safely in the protective white coat of the doctor), or perhaps you have replaced it with 'sufferer' (diminishing the control of the person with AIDS over their life and over their experience of living with this illness).

Through careful listening we can begin to attune ourselves to what familiar words mean to our friend and learn how to speak so that our words have meaning for him.

We have made ourselves available; waited; and eventually been called in. We have entered in Christ and recognized Christ in our friend. We have tried to hear how our friend understands the Christ in him and to speak to him in terms which ring true to his experience. The healing process has begun.

Healing

Healing is three-way. It heals the person who perceives himself as sick and his relationship with God; it heals the physician and his relationship with God; and it spills over to heal those who come into contact with 'patient' and 'healer' – not only people and animals, but also the environment. It is significant that mission and healing share a common definition: reconciling humanity with God, with each other and with the natural environment. It follows from all this that we are all 'patients' and all 'healers'. We are all partly broken and partly mending. We go into the sick room to heal and to be healed.

What we bring with us

No one comes empty-handed into a sick room. For our own protection as much as to show our love, we come bearing gifts, often reflecting our needs rather than those of our friend. Some of these gifts take the form of stories.

There is the story of our relationship with this friend before he came into hospital. There is the story of our other experiences of this illness, perhaps also involving the story of someone else we knew who had this illness. There is the story of our own feelings about being ill ourselves. There is the story of our own feelings about our death.

We may not be able to leave them outside with any other inappropriate gift that may be harmful to the sick person, because they are part of us. But we do need to be aware that we have brought them with us.

They are less likely to come between us and our friend if we reflect that we may have brought these stories with us because they represent parts of us that need healing. We should therefore not try to put them out of our minds, but reflect on them before we enter the sick room, so that once we do enter we can be empty of ourselves in order to be full of our friend.

What we invite in to distract us

The hardest thing in a sick room is to keep still and not be embarrassed by being still; to be aware of our sense of frustration at not having something to do, yet not give in to the temptation to make ourselves busy. Patting pillows and tidying bedside tables, fiddling with temperature charts and smoothing counterpanes – even drawing attention to the flowers, books, fruits and toiletries we brought along – these must be resisted.

Place them quietly as a gift. Note what is still needed and remember to supply that need – unnoticed – on our next visit. Then settle down comfortably, close enough for our friend to speak without straining, and for us to speak without being overheard. And wait. And listen.

I love you

All we have to offer is our love. A kiss and a hug show it, but it does help also to say it. So let the silence settle and drop into it these words. If the silence continues – for example, if our friend is in a coma – use the silence to reflect on why we love our friend. We are able to love him because we have accepted that we too are loved. It is God's love for me that sparks off my loving myself and builds up my sense of my own loveableness. It is my loveableness that enables me to see and respond to the loveableness in you and helps me, in time, to say, 'I love you'.

The silence of 'loving-waiting' is so expectant it can thrill, so charged with harmony it can reverberate between people and transform a noisy hospital ward by filling it with a new music. We discover in that silence of 'loving-waiting' that there are other and better ways of communicating than through speech or touch.

The hand

We are here to offer and to accept healing, not to demand it. So when we offer our friend our hand, we do so in such a way that it is placed within his grasp, held palm outward close to his, so close our skins can feel the warmth of each other's presence. But we do not grab or squeeze his hand. We cannot force even our love on to him. We can only offer it.

As we look down at our hand in this position, we are reminded that this offering of ourselves is all we can or should do. If our friend is comatose, we can close his hand between both of ours, but only gently. He is ultimately other than us. We cannot take his pain into ourselves or do any more than try to understand how he feels about his pain.

And when and if words come, they are like this touch: tentative, proffered, lightly started, quickly dropped as our friend chooses to pick them up or lay them down.

The eye

Clearing the space between you, both of your favourite distractions and of your hidden agenda, has one further advantage. It allows you to see your friend more clearly. He is no longer caught up and entangled in a projection of your own fear and hopes for yourself. He is separate. He is other than you. He has his own identity, his own integrity, his own space. You are no longer seeing him as you wanted him to be, the sort of friend you thought you had. He is his own.

It may well be you like him less now you see him as a person and not as a person with AIDS. It may well be that you are now strangers to each other. That does not matter. You have found Christ in you and you have sought Christ in him. That is enough to bind you for now. Perhaps it is more than bound you before. Clear-sightedness is what you will need next, and what this process gives you.

You will need clear-sightedness because you have created a vacuum between your friend and yourself by taking away those things which do not properly belong to your friend. In that vacuum hangs God.

You and Christ within you now both wait on your friend and Christ in him. God waits with you and on you both, suspended like hoar frost on your breathing out, freely flowing in and out of you as you breathe.

Into that vacuum your friend can pour his deepest trouble and his lightest thought. You will need consciously to welcome and accept each of his concerns as he presents them, knowing that you are three friends sharing secrets in a midnight feast.

Because we are none of us used to being given time to say all that is on our mind fully and without the need to be careful or quick in how we express what concerns us, not everything he says may necessarily be literally true even for him. At first it may be his attempt to translate his worries into terms you will – he hopes – understand or expect. Accept what he says and give him time to go deeper, to cancel or correct, or to just leave floating a sentence half-begun.

You will not feel shocked or frightened or embarrassed by what he says if you remember that he is not just sharing it with you. Remember the image of the friends swapping secrets in a midnight feast: there are three of you and God does not want your littleness of understanding to interrupt his conveying to your friend how much he really understands and accepts and loves your friend.

Perhaps your friend has a macabre fascination to the point even of obsession with the minutiae of death or with the process of bodily decay. How will my corpse be cleaned? What will the people who sponge it down be thinking of? Talking about? How will they get my body out of the ward without anyone else seeing it? What is a mortuary like? What if I'm not really dead? Will there be a post-mortem? Will my body be sealed in a plastic bag for anyone to stare at? Will an undertaker be found or, because of what I have died of, will my body just be dumped outside the mortuary door? Or was that story apocryphal? Will my body be cremated? Will I have the choice? Who will decide for me? Who, if anyone, will mourn?

Accept these questions. Ask what he wants. How would he treat his body if he were the nurse laying it out? How would he want his remains to be disposed of? In what clothes? Does he want to make up a list of people to be notified of his death and invited to his funeral? Does he have a particular vision of how that occasion should be celebrated? How does he want to be remembered?

The ear

Listen to what he says. Note it. If the occasion arises – because he has raised it – come back to it. Repeat to him what he said on this occasion and find out if he still feels the same. Help him to refine what he wants so that it is clear to him. Don't volunteer fulsome promises you can't deliver. In all probability he is not asking you to do anything, just to let him get something off his mind so that he can get on to something more important, something he wants to say without interruption, contradiction, distraction or any gnashing or wailing on your part.

It may be that once this discussion of the physical aspects of death is out of the way, he will want to go on to talk about how he survives death. Perhaps not. Perhaps he only raised the subject in this way to test you or to test himself: to exorcize a spirit of fear, to talk away a nightmare.

Exorcisms played a significant part in Christ's healing ministry and we all have spirits within us that need banishing in the name of Christ. But don't wade in with bell, book and candle – just be aware of what is happening inside him and inside you.

However, if you responded to his outpourings with horror or, worst of all, with an air of martyred Christian forbearance, you – not he – will have created a gulf between you which he may never again invite you to bridge. He knows how much and how little energy he has left and will want to expend it only on and with people who truly accept and are with him.

Acceptance

Acceptance may well be the key to understanding and coping with his many changes of mood and subject matter. The fact that he is picking up and discarding topics so quickly should give you a clue as to how restless or restful he feels inside; to whether he is accepting or resisting God, the disease and himself; and as to whether he sees himself as potential victor or actual victim.

If your friend sees himself as a victim of AIDS, try to find out why. Explore with him, if he will let you, why he – or is it you? – sees himself as a victim and what this means in terms of his self-acceptance. Observe what effects this 'victim' feeling is having on the progress of his illness. Have you both unconsciously accepted that this time in hospital is his last?

Helping your friend see that he is of worth, neither despite nor because of AIDS, will help prevent him from hiding behind AIDS from facing the truth about himself. And that truth must contain the fact that he is worthy of love because he is loved; that he deserves life because he has been given life; that he is accepted by God as he is and unconditionally loved by God.

But the starting point for this has to be our belief in our own worth, our experience of being loved. From this starting point we go on to believe that life is a precious gift to be lived to the full. We realize that life's value is in its quality not its quantity; in the enjoyment of repaired relationships regardless of still sick bodies.

Since it is not God who is withholding love, it follows that it is often the person withholding himself from being accepted, forgiven, loved and thereby healed. Healing can finally come only to those who want it.

Healing

Which brings us back to healing. The healing Christ offers is one which restores us to right relationships; that assures us of his presence in our sufferings, but does not promise an escape from that suffering – an escape even he was not granted.

This sort of healing allows us to trust that not even our death will separate us from life in all its fullness, life in him. Nor is this a hope for a distant 'hereafter': Christ's healing is something we experience now, his heaven one we are invited to enjoy in this life as well as in the next.

Our friend's sense of separation – from his body, his family, friends and society – is the starting point for that healing. Our awareness of apartness, of alienation, points to the root cause of our real illness in our broken relationships. Healing is the experience of God's help to re-create in us a new sense of real unity with our body; the building of new bridges in our relationships with those we already know and love, this time based on loving mutual acceptance; a coming together with society, this time based not on any pleading for a right to belong, but with the authority of one sent as a messenger from God to proclaim what John Fortunato has called 'the good news of our mortality'. Most of all, that healing will be experienced as a new sense of at-one-ment with God.

In this part of the book, I have tried – I fear neither wisely nor well – to show what will be distinctive about Christian ministry to people with AIDS. It will be characterized by attitudes of patient waiting-on, of offering but not forcing oneself in love to the other person, while respecting their 'otherness'. It will show itself in finding ways to understand and speak the language of our friend and helping him (if we are invited) to know himself loved. It will offer him – and receive from him – that healing which restores us to full communion with one another and with God, as we come to accept that we are worthy of love simply because we are loved and that we deserve life in all its fullness simply because that is what God offers us.

In the end, the whole purpose of Christian ministry to people with AIDS is that no one should die in ignorance of the fact that God loves us.

Material for prayer and reflection

It is at this point that readers really need to come together with their friends to share how they are going to respond practically to AIDS.

What can your local church do to make people affected by AIDS feel welcome and accepted with you?

What can your local churches, working together, do to support existing local voluntary AIDS groups?

What are you going to do personally?

– ring the National AIDS Helpline and make contact with your local AIDS group

– find out what their current needs are and decide how you can help to meet some of those needs

– contact one of the national AIDS Christian organizations and link your prayers into theirs.

It is always possible that your offer of help will be rejected. When this is the result of others' suspicions of your Christian motives, this can be particularly hard to bear. Re-examine your motives. If you are hoping to convert someone or to 'adopt a person with AIDS', or if you feel you have all or even some of the 'answers', they are right to reject you. If you have come to offer yourself, to listen, to learn and to share, then keep trying.

Recommended reading:

Bill Kirkpatrick, AIDS: *Sharing the Pain*, Darton, Longman and Todd 1988.

Prayer

Help us to accept the challenge of AIDS:
to protect the healthy, calm the fearful;
to offer courage to those in pain;
to embrace the dying as they flow into love's unendingness;
to console the bereaved;
to support all those who attempt to care for the sick and the dying.

Enable us to offer our energies,
our imaginations,
and our trusting in the mysteries of love,
to be united with and through one another
in liberating each other
from fear of this disease.

We offer these thoughts and prayers
in the mystery of the loving
that can and does bear all our woundings,
whatever their source,
through the spirit of love's concern
for each and every person. Amen

Written by Bill Kirkpatrick and quoted in his book, AIDS: *Sharing the Pain*.

Letting Others Love Us

Letting Others Love Us

Introduction

Part Four is concerned to show that our ministry to people with AIDS is only one side of the coin. Their ministry to us is at least equally as important, for it is the means by which we too are healed and our capacity to enjoy and value life is enhanced.

Some of the things we can learn from people affected by AIDS include how to live each moment consciously in the presence of God, awakened to this by a new awareness of the fragility and preciousness of simple existence; how our own healing is worked out through our working to heal broken relationships; how to acknowledge and deal with our own unfinished business; how to acknowledge and cherish what matters most in our life; how to forgive and love ourselves so as to be freed and enabled to forgive and love others, even those in the Church who sometimes appear to be persecuting us.

Part Four is very short because I believe we must each discover for ourselves what we need to learn from people affected by AIDS and from the experience of being alongside the Christ in them. It is perhaps a chapter to which readers may want to return over the years and to use as a sort of touchstone as their experience grows.

Letting others love us

We began this book by acknowledging our mutual need of forgiveness and healing, whether or not we personally have AIDS. But we then went on to look at how as Christians we can minister to people with AIDS. Now we must redress the balance so as to preserve the truth: that our mutual healing will come through our mutual ministering. It is so much easier to offer love than to receive it that we may be tempted not to recognize the other side of the coin. On the one side is our ministering to people with AIDS, but on the other side is the equally (if not more important) ministry of people with AIDS to us. This is the exciting side, the new side, the side which will transform our perceptions of our world and our purpose in it. But if we are to learn from AIDS, we shall have to be taught by those who have AIDS.

There is a divine irony in the way that those whom society has judged accursed are now to be bearers of blessing; those whom society has condemned should be the means of the healing of that society; and those whose life-styles the church has denounced should be the very ones chosen to announce how we should live our lives.

Nor should this surprise us. The Bible is full of such pointers. When Samaria was being besieged by Ben-hadad and the king was at his wits' end, he sent to the prophet Elisha for advice. Elisha promised that within twenty-four hours 'a measure of fine meal shall be sold for a shekel, and two measures of barley for a shekel, at the gate of Samaria', but the idea seemed so preposterous that everyone scoffed and no one believed him. As we feel ourselves besieged by what we perceive as the plague of AIDS, we too are incredulous at the idea of any good coming out of it, any healing to be found within it, so perhaps we should look more closely at this story, which is recorded in II Kings 7.1–20.

It tells of four men who were lepers. They had nowhere to go: they had retreated from the besieging Syrians as far as the entrance to the city gate but because they were unclean they would not have been allowed into the city. They were in no man's land, rejected by both sides.

So they decided to try and walk through the Syrian lines. If they made it, there might be food to be found on the other side. If they did not make it and the Syrians killed them, a quick death seemed preferable to the slow death of starvation. Either way, they wouldn't need to worry about hunger again.

They approached the Syrian camp at twilight and to their amazement found it quite deserted ('For the Lord had made the army of the Syrians hear the sound of chariots, and of horses, the sound of a great army . . . so they fled away in the twilight' (vv.6, 7)). Realizing their good fortune, the four lepers plundered the Syrian tents, then ate and drank their fill. But they felt it would be wrong to keep the good news to themselves. The people in the city would not have thought to share the good news of their release with the lepers had they been first on the scene and would certainly not have shared the benefits with them. Nothing would alter their outcast state. But perhaps knowing what it was to feel hopeless, they could not let the people of the city dwell another night in their hopelessness. They said to one another: 'We are not doing right. This day is a day of good news . . . let us go and tell the king's household' (II Kings 7.9). So the prophecy came true, the people celebrated their salvation . . . but there is, interestingly, no mention of their thanking those who brought the good news.

God's good news always seems to come from the most unexpected sources, brought to us by least-esteemed members of our society – barren women, old childless men, lepers, unmarried virgins, the illegitimate (in society's eyes) sons of carpenters from the most despised places ('Can anything good come out of Nazareth?' Philip asks, according to John 1.46).

So the challenge to us is not just to find and recognize Christ in people with AIDS but to ask them how the works of God are being made manifest in their experience of AIDS: 'It was not that this man sinned, or his parents, but that the works of God might be made manifest in him' (John 9.3).

Is there any way in which that can be said of the person with AIDS? It sounds preposterous. Yet I wonder. At a time of deep crisis in a civilization, an apocalyptic time, an 'end-time', it does seem that some people have to sacrifice more than they would choose to do – and on behalf of others. This is an interpretation that cannot be forced on anyone, but some might be able to choose to accept it. May it be that a few people, symbolically suffering that universal death that we all fear, can make us look that death more clearly in the face, feel the fear, allow it to melt inside us, and so let it become a power of love and will to make some sacrifices of our own for the sake of the earth's survival – sacrifices of time, energy, wealth – so that this world may come through the death-throes of an old order and the birth-pangs of a new one? The gateway to life has always been through a dying, both as individuals and as representatives of humanity. There are echoes here of the Suffering Servant of Isaiah 53 and of Christ on the cross. These are deep waters indeed, but they may need to be stirred, however gently and cautiously.

Jim Cotter, *The Other Country*, Cairns Publications 1985

It is only from those with AIDS that the answer can come. All we can do is to help them see the possibility that their 'election to suffering' contains an opportunity for them to experience before us a message of salvation from the fear that is besieging us, and to plead with them not to keep that experience to themselves but to share the good news with those of us still walled up within the city of our mortality.

Material for prayer and reflection

Walking on water

This is a simple visual meditation on the story of Jesus walking over the water to his disciples and inviting them to do the same. Read Matt. 14.22–33. Study the picture and see whom you recognize. The notes under the picture may or may not help you. Discuss your findings in your group.

1 2 3 4 5 6 7 8 9 10

1. Some will only think and 'theologize'.

2. Some will only wonder and keep at a distance.

3. Some will only pray and thereby fail to see where practical help is also needed.

4. Some will refuse to see, think or pray.

5. Some will dive straight in where hope is already lost . . . and lose themselves as well.

6. Some will need help but refuse it.

7. Some will need help and accept it.

8. Some will give support and see that they also need support.

9. Those who are exhausted with giving can be supported by others even though they do not realize they are being helped.

10. All of us are needed both to give and to accept support if the chain of God's loving concern for his people is to ring the world.

A Litany of Reconciliation

Almighty God, creator of life, sustainer of every good thing I know, my partner with me in the pain of this earth, hear my prayer as I am in the midst of separation and alienation from everything I know to be supportive, and healing, and true.

AIDS has caused me to feel separated from you.
I say, 'Why me, what did I do to deserve this?' . . .
Help me to remember that you do not punish your creation
by bringing disease, but that you are Emmanuel, God with us.
You are as close to me as my next breath.

AIDS has caused a separation between the body I knew and my body now . . . Help me to remember that I am more than my body and, while it pains me greatly to see what has happened to it, I am more than my body . . . I am part of you and you me.

AIDS has separated me from my family . . . Oh God help me and them to realize that I haven't changed, I'm still their child, our love for each other is your love for us . . .
Help them overcome their fear, embarrassment and guilt . . .
Their love brought me into this world . . . Help them share as much as possible with me.

AIDS has caused a separation between me and my friends; my friendships have been so important to me. They are especially important now . . . Help me oh God to recognize their fear, and help them to realize my increasing need for them to love in any way they can.

AIDS has separated me from my society, my work world and my community . . . It pains me for them to see me differently now . . . Forgive them for allowing their ignorance of this disease and their fear to blind their judgments . . . Help me with my anger towards them.

AIDS has caused a separation between me and my Church. . . . Help the church restore its ministry to 'the least of these' by reaching out to me and others . . . Help them suspend their judgments and love me as they have before . . . Help me and them realize that the church is the Body of Christ . . . that separation and alienation wound the body.

God of my birth and God of my death, help me know you have been, you are, and you are to come . . . Amen

Author unknown: quoted by Bill Kirkpatrick in AIDS: *Sharing the Pain*

Recommended reading:

Walter J. Smith, SJ, AIDS: *Living and Dying with Hope*, Paulist Press, New York 1988.

Letting God Love Us

Letting God Love Us

Introduction

Part Five draws together the themes of the book and asks what we have learnt about ourselves and others through making the momentous decision to serve Christ in our neighbours who have AIDS.

It is very much in the form of a meditation because its purpose is to show that prayer is the way we link up our own and our friend's pain with the pain-bearing God; how through prayer we are healed and empowered to heal. It explores some of the new things we have discovered about God and about being his children and it suggests that this has enriched our lives and broadened our capacity to understand others. What began as a simple but painful question about a virus ends in bringing us closer to God and to each other. Our work with people affected by AIDS becomes part of our prayerful pilgrimage to the source of all Life.

Letting God love us

'Watch and pray that you may not enter into temptation; the spirit is willing, but the flesh is weak' (Matt. 26.41).

In that Garden of Gethsemane which is AIDS, we are again reminded how different are our respective roles. To the person living with AIDS belongs the sensation of a soul 'sorrowful, even to death' (v. 28); the entreaty in blood and tears that they should not have to drink from the cup of suffering to its deathly dregs –

'nevertheless, not as I will, but as thou wilt' (v. 39). To the person who cares for them belongs the duty of watchfulness and prayer.

Watchfulness was an urgent theme in the final stage of Christ's teaching. 'Watch, therefore, for you know neither the day nor the hour' (Matt. 25. 13). Watchfulness is not only alertness to God at work in our world, but preparedness for the moment of his coming. Traditionally, Christians have understood this coming as happening at our individual death and at his Second Coming in glory to judge the world. But some Christians have felt what might be called tremors – anticipatory experiences of his 'gathering in' – at significant points in their lives.

This is perhaps appropriate because in Matthew's Gospel these calls to be prepared for his Second Coming are bound up with the teaching on our duty to feed, welcome, clothe and visit those in need, upon which so much of our thinking in Part One was based.

But with this warning and reminder of our duty come also promise and assurance: 'But he who endures to the end will be saved. And this gospel of the kingdom will be preached throughout the whole world, as a testimony to all nations; and then the end will come' (Matt. 24.13, 14). The promise is that if we remain faithful, we shall be saved. The assurance is that the salvation we have accepted will also have been offered to all peoples in all places. We are called to alertness to the sound of his voice, watchfulness for sight of his activity and wakefulness to respond to his call – whenever it comes, whatever it bids us do.

This is where prayer comes in. Prayer is the whetstone against which we sharpen our spiritual wits; the splash of cold water that refreshes and restores us to wakefulness. Prayer is the way we consciously and constantly check our 'in-step'-ness, our harmony with his rhythm.

But our prayer in the Garden is quite specific: it is prayer for ourselves, prayer that we 'may not enter into temptation'. The temptations of working alongside people with AIDS are many and varied – as varied and many as we are. But among them may be these:

Temptation to despair

Hopelessness fills the air. We feel suffocated by despair. Whatever we do, people die anyway. What is the point?

We have to remember that we shall all die 'anyway'. Our coming alongside people with AIDS is not to prevent them from dying but to offer them the chance to experience what it is like to taste life in all its fullness, to know how much God loves us. If we feel loved, needed, valued and accepted, then our fears of dying will at least be put in perspective and our dying can become like our living: an experience of the closeness of God.

A feeling of uselessness

We must be careful to part the fibres of this one a little. Whose uselessness do we mean? Our own?

If what we are doing is what we believe God wants us to do, then we are being supremely useful simply by being obedient. Anyway, the words 'useful' and 'useless' are not in the Christian dictionary, because we are not finally called to do anything but to be someone: ourselves as God wants us to become. All our 'doing' is therefore only a reflection of all our 'being'.

But perhaps by 'useless' we mean 'inadequate'. We have to ask ourselves if this sense of inadequacy is about who we are or about what we have to offer. If it is about 'who I am' then I have to remember that God made me and loves me as I am, so I need to learn to accept and love myself as part of my co-operating with God, who is working in and with me in order to make me more fully in his image.

If my feeling of inadequacy is about what I have to offer, then it can be positive and valuable because the frustration this feeling causes helps to keep me broken and vulnerable and therefore malleable to him, humble to his working in and through me.

But often the sense of uselessness is not expressed by the carer but by the person living with AIDS at a point when they are severely incapacitated by their illness.

It is one of the obsessions of our age that people judge their worth in terms of their usefulness. We have been encouraged by politicians and others to believe we are only really useful members of society when we are young and employed, relying on no one's help but our own. This political indoctrination must be challenged by Christians, for it is poles apart from the Christian idea of mutual dependence. Christians believe we all need each other and that we all need God. For Christians the person with a mental handicap is just as useful (necessary) as anyone else. The old person in retirement is just as useful (valuable) as anyone else.

Of course it is easy to understand how someone who is totally dependent on medical drugs and machines just to stay alive can come to feel useless in the sense of feeling they have nothing to contribute. But our worth comes not from anything we do but from the fact that we are loved. If even in this utter state of 'uselessness' we can feel loved by God, and those whom we love still show how much they care for us and how much we matter to them, then, as Jim Cotter writes, we are close to experiencing how 'love might be the power that moves the universe'.

> Useless?
> Is this where we go wrong?
> Are we so attuned to the values of the age
> that we judge only by results,
> only by usefulness?
> . . .
> But maybe that's a sign –
> being useless.
> For if I'm loved in that precise condition,
> not respected,
> not needed,
> not able to give,
> then love might be,
> might be,
> the power that moves the universe.
>
> Jim Cotter, *Healing – More or Less*,
> Cairns Publications 1990, p. 21.

A feeling of exhaustion

This is far and away the most common malaise among carers and often is a symptom of one of these other dis-eases. When you feel it coming on, remember what Jesus said: 'Learn from me: I am gentle . . .' We do have to be gentle with ourselves, not pushing our bodies or our minds to extremes. If it helps to see your body as an instrument in God's service, then it behoves you to look after that instrument. In the parable of the Wise and Foolish Virgins, the difference between wisdom and folly lay not only in wakefulness

126

but also in care of the lamps. Our bodies are those lamps and we do have to look after them.

But sometimes exhaustion is not related to anything else. On these occasions it often comes when we try to look ahead and all we can see is more suffering, more work, more pain. Here it helps to remember that we are called to live in today, not regretting yesterday or fearing tomorrow, but seeing today as the only moment we have to enjoy and use for God. Waking up in the morning and immediately repeating a phrase like this might help:

This is the day the Lord has made;
let us rejoice and be glad in it.

But sometimes exhaustion is the reaction to seeing ourselves at the centre of all the giving. 'Look at all this work I must do because if I don't do it no one else will.' This really is the Christian cancer. It creeps into our consciousness so insidiously that by the time it has established itself we are reciting it as a creed and unable to see its malignity. The work is God's. He is doing it. He asks us to come alongside and help him out – not take over, not do it on our own, not do it for (ie in place of) him. In a very real sense we are only called to watch him at work.

Where our help is needed, it is as a cog in a machine. A cog is only 'useful' if it works in perfect partnership with all the other cogs. So a useful starting point when we see someone in need is to make a list of all the needs this person has; which of these s/he wants and can do for themselves, which are being done by others, which are left over. Then look again at those which are left over and ask who you know has that particular skill. You will find yourself choosing those people who seem most relaxed. The job which needs doing may be to get the sick person's shopping. You know that they will not want someone who will rush in, grab the shopping list, dash to the nearest supermarket and get the first thing that comes to hand, dash back and dump them on the table. Not only will their racing about disturb the sick person, it will also make the sick person feel guilty at having added to the burden of someone who is so obviously short of time. Nor does this racing about help the carer. It only reinforces their sense of being in a rush. This breathlessness is a spiritual not a physical problem. The Hebrew word which we translate as Spirit is also the word for breath. In Genesis 2, life came

127

to dust when God breathed his breath into that clay and made it human, made it alive. So if we feel breathless, what we really should be recognizing is that we are Spiritless. What we need more than anything is deep breathing, deep praying.

So when exhaustion is caused by tiredness, rest and be gentle with yourself. When it comes from worrying about tomorrow, remember we are given only today. When it comes from thinking 'I' have to do all the caring, remember 'I' am only one cog and my usefulness is determined by the extent to which 'I' co-operate with God and with all the other cogs. But when exhaustion is the result of finding the weight of our particular task too great, reflect on Jesus' offer: 'Come unto me all who labour and are heavy laden, and I will give you rest. Take my yoke upon you, and learn from me; for I am gentle and lowly in heart, and you will find rest for your souls. For my yoke is easy, and my burden is light' (Matt. 11.29, 30). It is the yoke we put upon ourselves that exhausts us; our determination to pull the burden alone that wears us out. But a yoke is usually a device for helping two beasts to pull one burden. We are never required to pull alone.

A feeling of anger

Once you have overcome your own fears of contagion, your ignorance of this disease, your uneasiness with the questions of sexuality and mortality which it brings; once you have been trained and put to work alongside people living with HIV infection and illness, you will become angry. You will hear so many true horror stories of people being told their HIV status in ways which are cruel and vindictive; of the lovers and families of such people totally rejecting them; of their neighbours shunning them and trying to force them out; of queer-bashers attacking them or their homes; of well-meaning preachers telling them their disease is a punishment from an angry God; of fair-weather friends fading away as they become more and more ill; of families who have kept away while they were living suddenly making an appearance when they are dying and taking over and excluding everyone who has stayed the course; of undertakers making the funeral arrangements traumatic; of families excluding carers and lovers from the funeral; of faithful lovers made homeless by faithless families; of bickering and in-fighting between

128

volunteers; of some people making money out of others' suffering; and of volunteers burning-out for lack of support and supervision.

How much more angry must God be! How much more sorely must his sense of justice be tried! But we should reflect that without all the reflection, prayer, training and experience we now enjoy, we could so easily have reacted in the same way as those who now make us angry. If we had known nothing of AIDS, how would we have reacted when our son or daughter came home and told us they were HIV +? How would we have coped with the double shock of perhaps learning for the first time that our son was gay and dying? What would we have decided to tell the neighbours when they asked why our daughter had died so young? How would we have felt about having someone living next door who was HIV +?

And so our anger turns to sorrow and our determination to share the real truth about AIDS is reinforced. The pain that is left behind, though, remains with us, a tiny sharing in the pain of God through which the world is being redeemed.

A feeling of anxiety

'Therefore I tell you, do not be anxious about your life, what you shall eat or what you shall drink, nor about your body, what you shall put on . . . For the Gentiles seek all these things; and your heavenly Father knows that you need them all. But seek first his kingdom and his righteousness, and all these things shall be yours as well. Therefore do not be anxious about tomorrow, for tomorrow will be anxious for itself. Let the day's own trouble be sufficient for the day' (Matt. 6.25–34).

This passage is the perfect one for a meditation at the beginning of yet another crowded day of caring. Living in today, trusting that in God all is working for good in those who believe, knowing that God will answer every need and provide every necessity: this is the answer to our anxiety.

But there are other temptations in this 'caring business'. Perhaps they will show clearer if they are described in character sketches. I am sure you will recognize several people you know in this list, but do remember that we can only recognize them because they are like us: they are less pictures than mirrors.

The AIDS maniac. This dervish zooms about doing, speaking, reading, eating, sleeping, talking AIDS at a pace that exhausts everyone else and makes the rest of us guilty that we cannot do as much, know as much, care as much as they appear to. But this person is manic and dangerous. Like any meteorite, they are liable to burn-out.

The AIDS martyr. 'I have chosen to share the lot of the lowest of the low', they say aloud, ('because I feel that's all I'm fit for', they add, so quietly they often do not hear it themselves). This leads to them living in a dreamworld, cut off from reality and is actually a form of self-rejection, of life-rejection. These people do not love themselves or value their own gift of life so they cannot love others or help them to value themselves. Their effect on the person with AIDS is depressing and no wonder – they are denegrating that person ('lowest of the low') and themselves. They need help.

The AIDS crusader. 'In the battle against this killer disease we must summon up our strength and arm ourselves for the fight. There is the Devil to do battle with. Sin to be conquered'. Such a person just cannot understand what it means to 'be with', to 'come alongside' someone with AIDS, in sharing pain, in patient waiting. They are exasperated when no progress is made, or blind to the real progress. They are defeated by death and in their defeat can bring down many others. They love the podium and the pulpit but must be made to realize they have nothing to teach and everything to learn. Keep them out of the limelight, away from the bedside. They will soon get bored and find another crusade to lead, but at least they will have done minimal damage to this one.

The AIDS statistician. This person knows all the facts, has read all the books (even this one, but not this page). They have all the jargon off-pat and would impress any AIDS specialist. They know the statistics but not the people. They know the numbers but not one of those numbers. They are on all the committees and courses, which they use to get themselves a job or promotion. But they rarely sit at a bedside and never rattle a collecting tin. Whether they have arrived at this position by fear of contact with suffering or by cynical opportunism, they are the real leeches: the ones who want to distance the people and live off the problem. They are the ones who, faced with a homeless person with AIDS, start a committee to found a hospice or a housing association (or a chain of inter-linked homes and hospices), but do not open their own heart or their own home. They find someone else to do the day-in, day-out grind of caring, while they pop in on alternate Sunday afternoons.

The AIDS myopic. This person seems to live for AIDS. They have few if any friends outside their local AIDS organization, no interests other than AIDS. But there is more to life than AIDS, more to suffering than AIDS. There are other problems in the world – all of them symptoms of the way in which our society has gone wrong, symptoms of the dis-ease of human beings.

The AIDS hypochondriac. Every carer I know has at sometime developed all the symptoms of AIDS. Fear of contagion is in all of us. The fact that someone has become a carer does not mean they don't have the usual fears of the rest of us, only that they try to overcome them. Sometimes the fear breaks through again. A sense of humour is the best cure because it allows us to laugh at ourselves and thus restore a sense of balance and perspective. (When my sister had her first baby – I had stretch marks for a month!)

But if you are persistently developing symptoms and know you do not have the disease, it is worth stopping for a while and taking some time away from all AIDS work to ask yourself if your body hasn't had enough. Sometimes our minds have strange ways of telling us they've done all they can and want to stop. There is no shame in this, rather it takes a lot of courage to realize that after a few months or a few years one has come to the end of all one can positively give for now. Nor does this mean the end of our usefulness.

Some people have only reached the end of their initial training when they reach this point. Others have befriended several people with AIDS over several years. They do not disappear from the scene. They become part of that caring accepting community which, after all, is the main thing we are trying to bring about – a society in which the fact that you are antibody positive or have AIDS simply does not matter.

So if you have reached this point, do not feel a coward or that you have given up. Go on to the new work God will show you, grateful for the way your sympathies have been enlarged, your own humanity

131

deepened, your own self more loved, more valued. Thank God for the part you have played, for what you have learnt and for making you, in every sense, fitter for the future.

With the exception of the AIDS hypochondriac, all the other 'masks' were means of self-defence and like most means of self-defence, were basically aggressive. The beautiful, balletic movement of T'ai Chi are merely slowed-down means of attacking someone. They give a sense of personal invincibility. In the end, the theory appears to go, you do not attack anyone because you are not afraid of being attacked. If anyone does attack you, you can do more damage to them than they can do to you. This cannot be the Christian approach. We cannot afford to put up any barriers to our vulnerability. We have to 'wear our hearts upon our sleeves', even for jackdaws to peck at.

While on a Shakespearean theme, we might pause to remember two equally dangerous approaches popular with Christians. They are what I call the Fortinbras and Hamlet approaches.

Fortinbras, you may remember, takes over where his father left off, conquers Poland and wins Hamlet's crown of Denmark, while Hamlet is still dithering about whether and how to avenge his father's murder (and getting himself murdered in the process). Fortinbras' life speaks his philosophy: 'Get stuck in' . . . to which Hamlet's life replies 'Yes I will, but I must think it through first.'

Both courses have dangers. To make most effective use of one's time and talents requires thought, but it also requires action. They are not opposites: action can produce the experience which refines the thought. So, for example, the Christian Fortinbras will be more effective in his new role if he takes time out to read this book. The Christian Hamlet, having read this book, should recognize that now is the time for action, not for more reading. Indeed, this book will make more sense a year after Hamlet has been doing the work. Then would be the time to go on to read the recommended books. This, by the way, is why there is only one recommended book per chapter: to encourage more thinking without allowing that thinking to fill all one's available time.

The temptations we have looked at all result from willing spirit and weak flesh. But prayer is the means of strengthening spirit to encourage flesh. Of course we shall fail: our courage, our energy, our endurance will falter. We shall, like the disciples, fall asleep.

But that must not be the excuse for giving up. So let us now look at how prayer can help to 'wake us up'.

Job's experience has already taught us a lot about how (not) to be carers to another's suffering. I believe he also has much to teach us about prayer. There are five points which spring immediately to mind.

1. There is nothing formal or restrained about how Job prays. He pours out his soul to God in a torrent of words. But also in days and weeks of silence.

2. The overriding characteristic of Job's relationship with God is one of utter honesty. He does not pretend to be pious: he is angry. When he hurts, he screams. In the face of mystery and silence, he is astonished. Sometimes he is 'looking for a fight'. Like Jacob, in prayer we can 'wrestle with angels unawares'.

3. The fact that Job's complaints are directed at God shows he does not want to break off his relationship with God. A lot has happened to rock his faith in God's justice and God's promise to protect him and he wants to sort it out. Sometimes we are too afraid or ashamed of our doubts to really face them. But doubts, when they are honestly faced and shared in prayer, can deepen faith. And if they don't, if faith is destroyed, then that faith was a seed sown on stony ground, or a house built on sand and the sooner it falls the sooner we can get on with the job of finding a firmer foundation for it.

4. Job's prayer proceeds from self-examination. Chapters 27 to 31 are a wonderful summary of his life and show how his life is rooted in his faith. Our self-examination, if it is as ruthlessly honest, full and open as his, will reveal just how central or peripheral our faith is to our living and may in itself reveal the source of the problem.

5. Such honesty (with himself and with God) obtains for Job a response from God: 'Then the LORD answered Job out of the whirlwind' (Job 38.1). The answer he gets is not for his comfort. It reminds him of his weakness and inconsequence by contrast with the power of God revealed in his creation. God demands: 'Where were you when I laid the foundations of the earth?' (Job 38.4).

God lists the creation of earth, sea, light, rain and the stars and then immediately contrasts these 'landscapes' with 'portraits'; he

133

sets these mighty elements side by side with pictures of great intimacy: 'Do you know when the mountain goats bring forth? Do you observe the calving of the hinds?' (Job 39.1).

God speaks of wild animals – ass and ox, ostrich, horse and hawk – and Job acknowledges his smallness, his being of 'small account' (40.4). God's transcendence and imminence, God's vastness and intimacy give Job – and us – a sense of perspective and a sense of awe.

In the most wonderful climax to any book in the Bible, we are reminded of the awesome majesty of God in the bizarre and the extraordinary, as God points for supreme proof of his creative power not to man but to Behemoth (the hippopotamus), not to angels but to Leviathan (the crocodile)!

The result? God and man are in dialogue. It is not going to be an easy relationship. It is full of questions on both sides, and perhaps of a realization by Job that his questions will only ever be answered by more questions; that he will have to wait for answers, cope with uncertainties, trust God to be in charge. It is the beginning of a dialogue between two adults and not between a father and a child, for out of all this pain Job has begun to grow. 'I had heard of thee by the hearing of the ear, but now my eye sees thee' (Job 42.5). We may not feel as Job does – 'Therefore I despise my self, and repent in dust and ashes' – but we will acknowledge that whatever we ask for in prayer we do get. In Job's case this is healing and restoration (Job 42.10–17).

So prayer is the natural activity of the believer. It is the continuing maintenance of contact with God through prayer that affirms our desire and God's desire to be in contact with each other. It is the means by which we come to understand God's will for us and at the same time the means by which God grants us *sight* of him.

The method of prayer is a sharing with God of how we are feeling about a situation, not only in words but also in silence, and always with complete honesty about our anger or hurt or bewilderment. To prevent us being caught up in the downward spiralling tornado of our pain, God points to his creative nature, not to destruction, and he selects the amazing and the bizarre in that creation. The zoo is therefore as much an aid to prayer as the ikon. We may well gain more insight into God and into our problem if we go to the zoo as well as to the church (and take your prayer group with you!)

But contemplation of God as Creator also leads us to reflect on our lives and on what we understand to have been our experience of God in our lives. This leads to contrition but also to a proper sense of our size and our worth, which in turn deepens our experience of his closeness to us and gives us a clearer insight into the ways in which he is working in our world, which will bring both enlightenment and heightened mystery.

If we start now to apply what we have learnt from Job, we probably find ourselves having to be honest in saying to God that the sort of healing we believe He is offering people with AIDS is not good enough. Possibly we can see that healing is more than just curing bodily disease, but we feel it has to contain that. Possible we can see that healing is more than a reward in the next life for suffering in this life, but we still feel that bodily healing should be demonstrable in this life. We have argued in this book that healing is a making whole of our sense of brokenness that restores us to communion and to community. As such, it can be experienced as much now as hereafter. Above all, it is a mutual healing. But even that seems unsatisfactory, incomplete.

Following Job's example, therefore, we bring to God in prayer the unsatisfactory feeling we have that the healing we offer and are offered is not enough. All right, it does restore to communion, but not to bodily health. All right, this was the same cup that not even Christ was allowed to pass up, but it still feels unjust, it still hurts.

We have to reflect that others will be praying with the same sense of offended justice to the same God, but from the opposite point of view. They see AIDS as God's curse on godless gays. They feel concerned at the unsatisfactory and incomplete nature of God's justice. They see no direct enough link between wrongdoing and punishment just as we see no direct enough link between repentance and healing. But to both of us perhaps God is saying the same thing.

If there were to be an incontrovertible direct link between action and consequence then there would be no need for faith, which is mankind's real lifeline. If one day a man announced he was gay and the next day he died of AIDS then we would only be able to respond to God in fear – the wrong kind of fear. If someone with AIDS one day asked God's forgiveness and the next day was cured of his AIDS, then we would only be able to respond to God in the wrong kind of certainty, with the wrong kind of faithful expectation of answer.

Either way faith itself would be destroyed because faith would be unnecessary.

Neither approach would help us to a clearer understanding of God's justice and healing. Nor would our experience of his justice or his healing be an experience of him – only, as it were, of a law of nature, of cause and effect. Nor would this experience lead us to realize how much we all deserve condemnation by his justice and depend utterly on the exercise of his mercy; how much we are all sick and need healing.

And it is in this realization of the universal and cosmic dis-ease of my personal dis-ease that a further truth becomes apparent. Just healing my personal dis-ease will not heal the dis-ease of my world, the dis-ease of which I would still be part. What I need is a way of offering up my suffering of my personal dis-ease for the healing of all dis-ease.

Awareness that our personal experience of disease is only a reflection of the disease in all of us, combined with willingness to offer the suffering of personal disease up to be used by God in the healing of all disease, is at least a beginning. Similarly, those of us not at the moment personally affected by AIDS can offer up our prayers for the healing of those we know with AIDS along with prayer for the healing of all the 'gone-wrongness' in our world.

Isaiah points to how this prayer can have effect when he reminds us that word-prayer is only part of action-prayer:

'Is not this the fast that I choose:
to loose the bonds of wickedness,
to undo the thongs of the yoke,
to let the oppressed go free,
and to break every yoke?
Is it not to share your bread with the hungry,
and bring the homeless poor into your house;
when you see the naked, to cover him,
and not to hide yourself from your own flesh?
Then shall your light break forth like the dawn,
and your healing shall spring up speedily;
your righteousness shall go before you,
the glory of the LORD shall be your rear guard.
Then you shall call, and the LORD will answer;

you shall cry, and he will say,
Here I am'

(Isa. 58.6–9a).

It is interesting to note the language Isaiah chooses to describe how healing is effected. It is a description of prayer in action. He does not speak in terms of battles, of conquering evil, of rooting out and destroying what is wrong in our society. He prefers to speak in terms of liberating (loosing bonds, undoing thongs, letting go free), and of sharing and protecting.

Our courage is certainly needed to see and address evil, but it is our gentleness and our loving concern, our capacity to put ourselves alongside and to share the shame of the naked and outcast with unstinting self-giving, that really answers prayer and thereby heals both people and their situations.

A man with several slipped discs sought medical advice. From a European doctor came the insistence on surgery. From a Chinese reflexologist came the suggestion of first trying gentle, firm massage to release the toxicity and to allow and encourage the body to heal itself. Perhaps Western Christians are too prone to react to the presence of evil violently and perhaps we can learn from Eastern Christians the gentler way of engagement. We have to live with evil and with the consequences of evil, but we do so with our eyes and hearts open and with our hands outstretched not clenched into fists.

This sort of 'healing – action – prayer' is not the gift or the ministry of a chosen few but is given to the whole people of God. That is why we need to find ways (for example, through prayer cells) of coming together to pray as well as to work for the healing of our world.

This sort of prayer allows us to see God creatively at work in the centre of that suffering, sharing it with us and using it as a means of drawing us closer to him. At least this way we actually experience the way he works and are comforted and encouraged by his presence, even if we do not understand his purpose in allowing that suffering at all.

Prayer is more than escape from what hurts us, it is a way in to understanding and dealing with why it hurts us. Prayer is more than our release from the burden of carrying that horror around with us, it is our means of engaging with the suffering that causes it.

What is common to these statements is a sense of mutuality, perhaps best described in terms of ebb and flow
 – between the demands placed on us and our response
 – between our needs and those of others
 – between our ministering and our being ministered to.

The effect of prayer, the result of healing, has its own set of symptoms, as had the dis-ease that led us back into prayer to seek healing. Through prayer, we grow less, we grow gentle, we grow in flexibility, and we grow in breadth of vision.

We grow less

'He must increase, but I must decrease' (John 3.30). The fact of our self-giving matters, the fact of the 'I' who does the giving does not matter. In fact, our 'busyness' or our sense of our importance can prevent or interfere with our being used by God. Like Job, we need to learn a new awareness of our littleness and our inconsequence. Beside this we need to place our growing awareness that it is Christ who is trying to grow in us and to shine through us. This will help us see we are not in the centre but on the edge of the ring. From that position we are better able to co-operate with him; to ascribe to him any praise that comes our way, aware that we are the means and not the end.

We grow in gentleness

'Take my yoke, and learn from me; for I am gentle and lowly in heart' (Matt. 11.30). This gentleness begins in our acceptance and treatment of ourselves, in the way we cherish and take good care of the bodies we have been given and which we have chosen to offer back to him for use in his service as instruments in his healing of his world. This self-gentleness can then rub off on others and express itself in gentleness of voice, of manner, of touch . . . so that our presence itself is soothing to be with.

We grow in flexibility

'Behold, I am the handmaid of the Lord; let it be to me according to your word' (Luke 1.38). We cease imposing on God or on others our own view of how we are to serve him and one another. While we wait to be of service, we do not stand stiffly to attention, but train ourselves in suppleness and speed of response. We watch and pray.

We grow in breadth of vision

We begin to see that there are no people with AIDS, only people. We see there is a need for hospital visitors, not for hospital AIDS visitors. We begin to see that AIDS is neither root nor cause but merely one symptom of the dis-ease of our society. We acknowledge that our own need to be healed is as great and as urgent as that of the illest person with AIDS.

The result is that we learn to flow with the river instead of seeing it necessary to wade across it, or worse, to battle our way upstream. We are, through prayer, learning to float, to trust God and our fellow-swimmers to hold us up. As we come to see activity as part of prayer, so passivity becomes meaningful. If our action is fuelled by love, then our inaction is the experience of being loved. We come to a curious calm in which we see our purpose in terms of enjoying being loved.

We come to a point when we sing with the Psalmist:

This is the day the Lord has made;
let us rejoice and be glad in it.

We are finally on this earth not to do (in the sense of 'achieve') anything, or even to be, but to be enjoyed by God, to give enjoyment to him by enjoying being part of his creation and by sharing that enjoyment with the rest of his creation.

We come to a point, as John Fortunato reminds us, of saying with the Preacher:

Go, eat your bread with enjoyment,
and drink your wine with a merry heart;
for God has already approved what you do

(Ecc. 9.7).

The Preacher goes on to tell us to enjoy life, to do 'whatever your hand finds to do' 'with all your might'. This is not passivity but receptivity: openness to the possibility of God and to his making use of what he puts our way.

So in prayer we have not only sought that everything should work to our good but found it to be doing so, and we have seen the small offering we make of our own suffering being used to heal all suffering, and in trying to love others that we are learning we are loved by him and learning how to let him love us more, to whom be the glory, both now and forever.

Material for prayer and reflection

Bearing more: bearing one another's burdens

Go deeper still into what healing is all about, and you discover a strange yet creative exchange among those who admit to each other that they are wounded. In the bearing of one another's burdens, in the sharing of one another's pain, we begin to dance.

. . .

Together we dance the dance of the crippled, crippled because, however fit and handsome, we are all far from being truly whole, yet a dance because in the midst of suffering we do give each other courage and joy, a sign that indeed one day all shall be well, broken bones shall joy, and with those very wounds we shall find that we have been made whole.

Abridged from pages 13 and 14 of the recommended book for this chapter: Jim Cotter, *Healing – More or Less*, Cairns Publications, 2nd edn 1990.